Praise for *Hope Unraveled: The People's Retreat*

"Over the past two decades, no one has been listening to the American people more attentively than Richard Harwood. This book eloquently summarizes what he has learned — the growing disconnect between the people and their political institutions, why it matters, and what we can do to begin turning the tide."

— WILLIAM A. GALSTON
Saul Stern Professor, School of Public Affairs, University of Maryland

"*Hope Unraveled* speaks to the heart of all Americans. It is an urgent call to recapture authentic conversations and connections in all aspects of public life — from our communities, to our schools, to our politics."

— CHAD WICK
CEO, Knowledgeworks Foundation

"*Hope Unraveled* offers useful insight into re-engaging the public. People want their voices heard and this book provides a way that the community can become involved in public policy."

— PAM IORIO
Mayor, Tampa, Florida

"*Hope Unraveled* is a testament to our times; to where we have come from, and to where we can go. It offers hope for the future. a way back for America"

— ANGELA QUINN
President, Boys and Girls Club of Las Vegas

"Harwood finds promise among public pathos and carefully extracts hope from impassioned pessimism. Here is a ringing endorsement of the public and political possibilities resident in the still strong foundation of the promise of the United States Constitution, the indefatigable strength of this nation, the content of Harwood's vision, and the substance of our civic hope — 'WE the people.'"

— C. WELTON GADDY
President, The Interfaith Alliance and The Interfaith Alliance Foundation

"*Hope Unraveled* should be required reading for anyone who wrongly argues that our nation is a house divided. Rich Harwood clearly articulates our common desire to believe in an America that is greater than the sum of its individual parts."

— BRET BICOY
President, Nevada Community Foundation

"Rich Harwood has an intuitive grasp of the spirit of America today. His keen analysis combines with his positive attitude about the power we have to influence our common life, to produce compelling reading for anyone who believes that we are not victims of 'the system.' We can make our own community — and our country — into the kind of place in which we want to live; Rich has the vision and track record to guide us in that process."

— REV. DR. DEBORAH KOHLER
Pastor, Woodside Church, Flint, Michigan

"Margaret Mead once said, 'Never doubt the power of a small group of individuals to change the world.' Rich Harwood in *Hope Unraveled* challenges you to join him in changing our world."

— JACK D. DALE
Superintendent, Fairfax County, Virginia, Public Schools

"*Hope Unraveled* digs deep, beyond the easy answers, to find the real reasons citizens have been in retreat from politics and public affairs. Rich shows his great listening skills and uses them to help us re-engage the public in the most critical of missions: that of taking charge of our own democracy."

— T. JAN WISEMAN
Executive Director, Greater Salisbury Committee

"In a society that puts so much stock in the big event, the silver bullet, the pivotal point, Hope Unraveled offers its antithesis: listening to each other as a way to find our common ground, to realize the public good. Politicians, pundits, and government officials take heed. Harwood has put his finger on the future. It springs up from a renewed sense of community, and it may well occur when you're not looking."

— GREGORY LEBEL
Assistant Professor of Political Management, The George Washington University

"This book chronicles the voices of America in a time of mistrust and hopelessness regarding the influence of personal involvement in politics and public life. Richard C. Harwood shines a light on a process to return hope for our future through true community engagement. This is a 'must read' for those who believe in collaborative decision making for the public good in neighborhoods, communities, states, and the nation."

— JOYCE E. BROOKS
Executive Director, Mahoning Valley Vision for Education

"In *Hope Unraveled*, Rich Harwood weaves a compelling narrative of Americans trying to make sense of our troubled public life. Sifting through 15 years of conversations, he deepens our understanding of the nation's mood and plots an inspiring course for renewal."

— MARLA CROCKETT
News Director, KERA 90.1

"Rich Harwood does the important work of holding up a megaphone to amplify the public's voice of discontent about our politics and community life. I know first hand how much the problems Rich outlines have undermined our collective ability to create effective supports for our youth. This book is an important read for anyone working to bring people together to solve public problems."

— KAREN PITTMAN
Executive Director, Forum for Youth Investment

"In these unsettling times, Richard Harwood has seen through the cynicism and mistrust and proposes an America that is once again full of possibilities and hope."

— RUTH WOODEN
President, Public Agenda

"Americans seem to have lost the art of listening, but Richard Harwood hasn't. For years he has been listening to — and hearing — the worries and concerns expressed across this land about our public life. *Hope Unraveled* engages the rest of us in this conversation, which has such enormous implications for a truly healthy democracy."

— DOROTHY S. RIDINGS
Former President and CEO, The Council on Foundations

HOPE

UNRAVELED

THE PEOPLE'S RETREAT AND
OUR WAY BACK

RICHARD C. HARWOOD

© 2005 by the Charles F. Kettering Foundation

ALL RIGHTS RESERVED

For information about permission to reproduce selections from this book, write to:
Permissions
Kettering Foundation Press
200 Commons Road
Dayton, Ohio 45459

This book is printed on acid free paper
First Edition, 2005
Manufactured in the United States of America
Design by Chris Lester, Rock Creek Creative
Library of Congress Cataloging-in-Publication-Data

Hope Unraveled: The People's Retreat and Our Way Back
p. cm.
ISBN 0-923993-14-2

*For Ray Rivers, an everyday hero
who taught me about hope*

TABLE OF CONTENTS

HOPE
UNRAVELED

THE PEOPLE'S RETREAT AND
OUR WAY BACK

FOREWORD

In 1990, the Kettering Foundation asked the Harwood Institute (then the Harwood Group) to look at the way Americans felt about their relationship with government and democratic politics. The results were reported in *Citizens and Politics: A View from Main Street*. In this study, Rich Harwood and his associates found that supposedly sovereign citizens thought they were being pushed out of their own political system.

Over the course of more than 20 years, Rich has made a substantial contribution by tracking the way people understand their role as citizens. In *Hope Unraveled*, a compilation of 15 years of research, his conclusions are as troubling if not more so than what he reported in 1991. Americans who felt pushed out of politics have become even more dispirited because of what they believe is a serious erosion of our sense of community and responsibility for one another. Citizens seem to have become more consumers than producers of public goods. They appear less inclined to look to themselves, and more disposed to look for leaders or heroes who will do for them what they don't think they can do for themselves. Confidence that citizens together can "overcome," whatever the odds, enjoyed a brief revival after 9/11, but waned soon thereafter.

Interestingly, this book coincides with the anniversary of another, John Dewey's *The Public and Its Problems*, which was based on lectures given in January of 1926. I say "interestingly" because Americans are still talking about many of the same issues. Dewey was contesting Walter Lippmann's argument that the public is merely a phantom of our political imagination. Dewey countered that the public is real but has difficulty recognizing itself and its powers. He wrote, "the outstanding problem of the Public is discovery and identification of itself . . . ." Then, with a nod to what he considered a source of the public's power, he added, "unless local communal life can be restored, the public cannot adequately resolve its most urgent problem: to find and identify itself."

The people Rich interviewed were implying something close to what Dewey was saying explicitly. The search for community seems to be either a continuing or at least a periodic preoccupation of American democracy. That is probably because our form of democracy took shape in frontier settlements where individual enterprise had to be balanced by social responsibility. Pioneers had to be both self-reliant and benevolent — willing to lend a helping hand. Reciprocity was essential to survival. The centrality of community in American democracy may also have had something to do with the necessity of building enough social cohesion to connect people pouring into the frontier from different countries, cultures, and classes.

American democracy still has its roots in communities where people, despite their differences, share time and a physical place — the most basic elements of common life. Democracy becomes an everyday experience as people respond to the things that happen to them hour by hour and in the particular spot on the planet that they all share. Today, we have other types of communities — based on identity, interest, and profession — but none of these seems to be a substitute for communities that are open to all people and serve all purposes.

Yet we may be losing these communities if Americans are retreating from civic life. People say they — and their neighbors — are pulling back. Even though they are a bit ashamed of retreating, they just don't see any alternative. They don't believe there are legislative remedies for the loss of community, and they don't look to political parties for some grand scheme to fix what has gone wrong in public life. The Americans Rich talked to were desperate to regain some control over their lives. So they were moving into close-knit circles of family and friends to find a "comfort zone." At the same time, they recognized they should and perhaps could reach out to others. And they were alarmed by what they saw as growing social fragmentation and extreme individualism. As one woman in Des Moines said, "people . . . have desires and goals for themselves, they don't have dreams and goals for the country."

Lest you find this retreat from community overly discouraging, look at the subtitle of Rich's book: *Our Way Back*. Reading between the lines of comments like those from Des Moines, I share Rich's optimism. The woman he quotes thought people *should* have dreams for the country. When others said they were frustrated because they didn't see any way to make a difference in combating the problems they worried about, they must have thought they *should* have been able to make a difference. And when people said they regretted the loss of community, they implied that community *should* be important. Even in the most recent interviews in this book, people say they should be doing more to join forces with others, which is one of the primary ways citizens have always made a difference. (Read the early history of the Civil Rights Movement, before 1955, and you'll see what I mean.)

Americans' sense of civic duty may not be completely dead. Sometimes people act on what they think they should do. In fact, they can be quite passionate about the need to make a difference in their community, for instance, when issues like the education of the next generation are at stake. In 1995, Harwood quoted a man in Portland, Oregon, who said to the people around him, "We sit here and we criticize public schools — they're awful, they're no good. But who the hell's going to change it?" Then the man answered his own question: "We are. We're going to change it. In your life you've got to do something. Everybody's got to do something." No wonder Rich worries when he hears people say they are no longer sure they can "do something."

Rich does more than worry, however. He has spent a good part of his career studying how people actually join forces to make a difference. What he found is quite surprising because he didn't discover a group of civic saints who put others' interests ahead of their own and stepped forward in a sudden and dramatic fashion to take up their civic obligations. Instead, he discovered that joining others is the culmination of a long process, which begins on a very personal level. Americans worry about *their* jobs, *their* health, and *their* children's education. And they keep coming back to those primary concerns, which remain as political touchstones. When people consider an issue, the first thing they usually ask themselves is, "Does this problem affect me or my family?"

This preoccupation doesn't mean Americans are totally selfish, however. If people see a connection between a community problem and their personal concerns, they are inclined to begin talking with other people to find out if they see the same connection. These conversations go on after church, in social gatherings, and during long rides home from work. People move in and out of a great many discussions, which are random and unstructured. Much of what they say may sound like small talk — with a lot of quaint stories thrown in. They are just mulling over what they hear or perhaps testing for a response: What did you see? What do you think it means? Does it worry you?

Later, town meetings might be held on what should be done about the problem at hand, and people would sort out their options — weighing each deliberatively in the best of circumstances. Some of the things they would decide to do might be done through ad hoc groups or civic organizations. Some might require action by government agencies. If these problem-solving initiatives result in citizens joining forces, a public begins to form with the capacity for more collective decision making and action. Working together draws people back into civic life.

Hope unravels slowly as communities lose social cohesion and people retreat into their safety zones. It also rebuilds slowly. But the way it rebuilds isn't by magic. We can help the recovery of hope along if we understand the process that Rich documents in the full body of his research. In fact, we all can "do something." And that is the most important insight that might be taken from this book.

Dr. David Mathews
President
Kettering Foundation

PREFACE

H *ope Unraveled* is about the American people today, their relationship to politics and public life, and our common task to foster authentic hope in the public realm. It comes at a time when many Americans have turned away from the public arena.

The book is based on a series of five distinct sets of conversations that my colleagues and I had in communities across America from 1990 through 2003. Every two years or so, we set out across the country under commissions by various sponsors to engage people in in-depth conversations about their thoughts, aspirations, and feelings for American life. In reporting the results of each set of conversations, I note the number of individual group discussions it consisted of and their locations. Each group conversation usually lasted between two and three hours and usually engaged 12 to 15 people randomly selected to represent a cross section of Americans by age, race, income, and education.

The aim of these conversations was to examine the relationship of Americans to politics and public life. I wanted to know why a relationship that is at the heart of democracy and community life in America today appears so devoid of possibility and hope — and how we might shape a different future.

WHERE WE ARE

ONE

The Great Challenge

C an you hear the people's voices?

What do they say about why so many Americans have turned away from politics and public life?

In my travels to towns and cities across the United States, I am often told the answer is that people are angry or apathetic, or lack the capacity, or maybe the interest, to engage in the world around them. Still another assertion is that people no longer care about each other, that they are unwilling to take the time to explore what they hold in common with their fellow Americans.

Yet another idea, this one quite recent, is that Americans have become politically divided. Anyone who tuned into the 2004 presidential race was regularly informed that the nation had become split between red states and blue states, signifying Republican and Democratic strongholds, respectively. Each day the news media would treat their audiences to an array of colored-coded maps graphically depicting this political divide. But in this case, no sooner had the 2004 election come to a close, when the pundits, pollsters, and political aficionados began to back-pedal, declaring that maybe the red/blue hoopla was just that — a lot of election-year hype.

Whatever the value of any particular notion, these and various other theories about why Americans have been turning away from the public arena, have often led to much hand-wringing and then to much speculation, even a bit of wishful thinking, about how to revivify people's involvement — or engagement, as it is commonly called these days. Such conversations can seem endless, sometimes tortuous, as they seek to reveal the hidden mysteries of human engagement in public affairs. But are these factors so mysterious after all? Is there something that people are trying to tell us that we fail to see and hear — and *know*? It seems to me that we often fail to look for a clear answer to the question, "What do the people's voices tell us?"

I have been traveling across America listening to people's voices for over 20 years. Each time I undertake a new round of conversations, I am reminded once more of the depth of people's concerns, the emotions embedded in their frustrations, and their enormous capacity to sustain hope that their condition will improve even as their fortunes seemingly take a turn for the worse. I can still vividly recall many of the people whose voices you will hear in these pages — where they sat in the room, what they said, the expressions on their faces, people from such diverse places as Des Moines and Philadelphia, Los Angeles and Dallas, Tallahassee and Seattle.

I believe these voices tell a story, and an important one. The voices speak about people's individual lives, and about the collective condition of the nation. By listening to them, we come to see why it is so difficult for Americans to engage in politics and public life. Understanding these voices can lead us to new openings and possibilities for making real progress in restoring involvement and trust in public affairs. Those of us concerned about our country's civic health are summoned to hear these voices and to act upon what they tell us.

But make no mistake. People these days resist engagement. Overcoming this resistance is a challenge that cannot be sidestepped. I consistently find in my work that many groups and organizations, while initially recognizing this challenge, seem to forget it once ensconced in their daily tasks or after encountering early victories that can lead to false confidence. Notwithstanding these efforts, or sometimes even because of them, we find in America today that people are reluctant even to believe in the possibilities of engagement. This is not, however, their wish.

THE RETREAT

I hope to show in this book that when it comes to people's relationships to politics and public life, something more widespread and troubling is taking place in the United States than is often recognized. The challenge goes far beyond the purported red/blue divide; it transcends efforts to analyze the problem from the perspective of urban or suburban or rural voters, or by categorizing people as church-goers and non-church-goers. Nor is it simply a matter of people being angry or frustrated about public affairs.

What ails us is felt throughout the land, among all the people, and strikes to the very core of our most cherished values.

Today, we face a trend that I believe is one of the most pressing challenges confronting this nation: Americans have been retreating from politics and public life into close-knit circles of family and friends. This retreat has only deepened and calcified over the years that I have been talking with Americans. Retreat is now a default position for many people; there seem to be no other relevant choices.

I do not claim that what I found in these conversations with Americans began abruptly in 1990, the time of my first set of discussions. Indeed, there has been an ongoing shift in how Americans view their relationship with politics and public life for decades. The findings from these conversations are obviously part of this larger social trend. But I believe I can fairly claim that my conversations point to an important juncture in this unfolding story — a time of citizen retreat from the public realm.

There are many individual reasons for this retreat. Here I underline the two that seem to me the most critical. One fundamental problem is that politics and public life have failed to address people's changing reality, leaving them with the feeling that they are on their own, without the confidence that their concerns will be addressed. The second reason is even more troubling and potentially more harmful: the actual distortion of people's reality, whereby people's concerns and hopes have been mercilessly abused or mangled in the daily iterations of politics and public life. The result is that people are unable to see themselves or their concerns truly reflected in the public square, and much of what they see seems unreal. In this way, people are robbed of the vital sense of coherence that we, as human beings, so urgently seek, especially in times of great change. People cannot find in the current public realm a sustained force for truth-seeking and the promotion of the public good. Noticeably missing is a sense of possibility and hope. In their place stands a politics and public life driven by manipulation, personal positioning, and material gain.

It is clear for many people that a politics and public life guided by coarseness and shallowness is now winning out, and as it does, there is a hole left in our society — an absence of humanity guided by a consciousness about what is meaningful and important to people in their daily lives.

But there is more to this story.

What we learn from people's voices is that instead of seeing the possibility of being active and engaged citizens, they have come to view themselves increasingly as consumers rather than citizens. They have become detached from their very connection and obligation to one another. They are, in a word, free-lancing their way through society, doing whatever they must to make ends meet and to pursue their individual dreams. A premium is now placed on making one's own way.

For many people, retreating from the public arena is the only way they believe they can gain a sense of control over their lives. As you will hear, many Americans say that they have too often abdicated their civic responsibility. And yet they can neither see nor imagine any recourse or alternate path.

WHAT IF EVERYONE LEFT?

The reason I have written this book is because I care deeply about politics and public life. I do not consider myself to be simply a neutral observer. Rather, I believe we all must actively find ways to engage ourselves and to engage our compatriots in the lives of our communities and our nation. People ought to have a place at the table of politics and public life. I have dedicated my entire career to this belief.

Further, my experience tells me that when the conditions are right, people will engage. What I find time and again as I travel the nation is that people want to step forward and join with others. They want to make a difference in society. Most of us want to do what is right and to be seen by others as being worthy of their respect. Most of us want to belong to something larger than ourselves. I see convincing evidence of such public impulses every time I engage a group of people in conversation and see the collective work they do in their communities. It seems clear to me that under the right conditions, these impulses can become active guiding principles throughout politics and public life. This said, my deepest concern is how such conditions may come to exist.

Let me take a moment here to underscore the importance of this challenge.

As you listen to people's voices in these pages, it becomes eminently clear that we as a nation must find ways to expand and enliven politics and public life; we *must*. For it is in the public arena that people shape their destiny and that of the larger society around them. It is there that we, as a society, identify and figure out common concerns, and wrestle with shared ideals — some of which have guided this nation since its inception, all of which are in a constant state of negotiation. It is through this public process that people debate different courses of action and try to determine the trade-offs they can live with. It is within the public realm that people forge relationships in the spirit of the public good, even while maintaining their individual identities.

But consider this scenario: What would happen if people were to decide they could no longer put their trust in the public realm; if their sense of connection with one another was so diminished and tenuous, they could no longer feel a part of something larger than themselves? What if people decided to remove themselves from the public square? What if the course of manipulation and personal positioning and material gain — of people engaging as consumers rather than citizens

— was, in fact, to win out?

I think most of us fear the answer to such questions because we already have a good sense of the potential outcomes — including more gridlock, acrimony, superficiality, unfettered consumerism, selfishness, and the growing manipulation and falsity of political life. My experience is that most people do not actively seek out such a future, even though, as we will see, their words and deeds, and those of others, may help lead them there.

The impending danger of such a scenario is sobering and troubling. For there is much work to do in our society — in ensuring, for instance, that every child receives a good education; that people can live in safe neighborhoods and in strong communities; that we find ways to improve race relations and rid ourselves of prejudice; that people have good health care and an adequate roof overhead. But such tasks can be achieved only through collective effort — through political or civic means — by individuals working together in some loosely-defined common pursuit. Absent a vibrant and robust politics and public life, such work stalls; it becomes mired in gridlock; it lacks an adequate sense of possibility and hope to propel it forward. At stake is the kind of society people want — the sense of values and connection and goodness that people yearn for.

A MATTER OF FUNDAMENTAL CONCERNS

The period from 1990 to 2003, when my colleagues and I crisscrossed the nation five times to conduct in-depth interviews with randomly-selected citizens, was one of tremendous *and* rapid change in the United States. Recall that it began with the end of the go-go era of the 1980s and the Reagan Administration, which was followed by the presidency of the elder George Bush, who promised a kinder and gentler nation. His one-term tenure, however, is perhaps best remembered for the decisive victory in the first Gulf War.

The early 1990s ushered in a deep recession, which was followed by the nation's greatest peacetime economic expansion ever, fueled in large measure by the burgeoning technology sector. The phrase "Silicon Valley" became synonymous with American ingenuity and prosperity. During this time, the popular use of the Internet emerged and with it the transformation of major segments of people's lives and of commerce, politics, and the world.

We also saw the rise and fall of Ross Perot and his United We Stand movement as well as policy debates over health care reform, welfare reform, campaign finance reform, and budget reform. This was not only a period of attempted reform, but also one of attempted redemption, as exhibited in the trials and tribulations of President Clinton, his impeachment, and his efforts to regain his political standing. This time period also heralded the dawning of a new century, and, along with it, the election of the second President Bush. Then, on September 11, 2001, the nation was rocked by terrorist attacks, which served as the precursor to war in Afghanistan and Iraq and initiated the larger war against terrorism.

Certainly no single study, or even a set of studies, could adequately cover a topic as important and sweeping as a people's relationship to politics and public life during so tumultuous a time. Nonetheless, I believe that this assemblage of voices at fixed moments over a period of some 15 years offers a clear view of people's fundamental concerns and the forces at work in their lives during these years; further, it reveals the significant challenges that we face in creating a vibrant and robust public realm in which people can find a place for themselves.

As you follow these conversations, do not expect to encounter the peaks and valleys of people's moods and views which we are now so routinely offered in public opinion survey data that instantly track responses to society's major events of the day. Obviously, these were tumultuous times. But what is so striking about these conversations is how they build in a clear and consistent manner over these years, despite the significant events that made news. They show that something deep and profound has been taking place in America's body politic. When taken together, these conversations reflect an *unfolding narrative* in America — a narrative about politics and public life that becomes increasingly ingrained with each passing set of conversations; a narrative that comes to inform people's views of society and shape their very views of themselves and those around them.

It is this *ingrained* narrative, about which I will have more to say in the concluding section of this book, that is so powerful in our politics and public today and that summons our urgent attention. Still, I do believe there is a way back from the people's retreat. In the final chapters of this book I suggest an alternate path for politics and public life which calls to us.

TWO

The Waiting Place

L et me set the stage with a brief sketch of what is to come.

As you listen carefully to the voices of the people with whom my colleagues and I spoke, you will enter what I call the "waiting place," a point in our collective history in which people see politics and public life as being stuck. It is a place where people are trying to make sense of the fast-paced changes encircling them; where they are longing for something good to happen to reverse the ill effects of change; where some, maybe many, are waiting for another opportunity to make the American dream their own. It is a place from which people find it hard to imagine a path outward toward the public arena.

You will hear people speak, with increasing clarity, about broken covenants, unspoken truths, unrecognized values, and the yearning for unsung heroes. These are the themes and forces that most clearly emerged from the conversations we conducted from 1990 to 2003. Again, I would not deny that they likely were present before the start of these conversations. Nor would I deny that there have been other times in American history when people have struggled with the meaning of the American experience. But in these conversations, we find these themes and forces coming together into a single powerful narrative as Americans struggle to understand their experiences and try to explain why they feel so thwarted in realizing their aspirations for the nation and themselves.

BROKEN COVENANTS

Listen to the people's voices in the following pages and you can hear them struggling to hold onto implicit covenants that have helped to form the essence of their lives, their sense of identity, and their place in American society. You will hear people speak of a time in their own lives when these covenants held — or, at least, for them, seemed to be in better shape. Their undoing now, has put at risk people's faith in politics, public life, indeed in themselves and in one another.

People do not speak expressly in terms of covenants; it is not a turn of phrase people use. But the concerns that troubled them the most profoundly went to the heart of how they related to one another, how they exercised their responsibilities and obligations, and whether they would reap the rewards of playing by the rules.

You will hear people initially raise these concerns in the early conversations. Then, with each subsequent conversation, one building on the other, you will hear people expand on them, a story of how politics and public life have failed to reflect people's reality and their deep desires for a meaningful response to their concerns.

Four broken covenants sit at the center of these concerns.

Lost faith in the American dream. Central to people's idea of the American experience is the belief that if you obtain a good education and work hard, you can get ahead. But over the course of this period, people expressed deep misgivings about a growing divide between the haves and have-nots; about corporate actions that suggested that workers were disposable and that corporate loyalty had become a value of the past; and about a shift in the employment of many Americans to lower paying jobs, which meant that people had to run harder just to stay in place. These changes led many people to question the meaning of the American dream and to wonder to whom it applies.

Free-for-all on basic values. People described a breakdown in the basic values that shape individual and family behavior in the nation. They complained that parents were failing to raise their children properly and were paying too much attention to economic and personal pursuits at the expense of their kids. They argued that the expectations of too many individuals, including themselves, were out of whack with reality; that people were unwilling to put in the necessary hard work and perseverance to fulfill their expectations; and that too many individuals were unprepared to sacrifice for others.

Materialism and consumerism run amuck. People increasingly said that an unrelenting greed and sense of materialism has overtaken many Americans, who have assumed the title of the almighty "consumer" — and expect to get what they want at the very moment they want it! An unrelenting focus on consumerism led some people to confuse the meanings of citizen and consumer, causing them to turn their backs on the public square, only to spend more time and effort frequenting the local shopping mall.

Breakdown in community. People saw a waning sense of community, and it deeply concerned them and offended their sensibilities. They lamented that many Americans did not seem to care about one another; were too often unwilling to help each other; and had built walls around themselves, with increasing numbers literally moving into gated communities. The expanded scale of society in terms of population and sprawl troubled many people. The old African proverb, "It takes a village to raise a child," was mentioned often in these conversations. In the eyes of many, this notion, which they saw as more necessary today than ever before, had been left behind.

These concerns — or broken covenants, as I term them — have had a profound impact on people. The rules of society are no longer clear to them; their ability to depend upon one another has been undermined; they feel isolated. They now believe that they must make their way in the world largely by themselves. And going it alone is what people have done. Amid these changes, people have chosen to keep their heads down, stay to themselves, and pursue their own dreams.

The vital connections that make up society are being significantly tested.

UNSPOKEN TRUTHS

Perhaps the most salient complaint people hold about politics and public life is this: that the public arena has utterly failed to reflect the reality of their lives. This abject failure has caused people to question almost everything they hear and see. Indeed, the deep skepticism that exists often borders on cynicism. If people once gave their leaders and fellow citizens the benefit of the doubt, now people withhold their support until leaders and fellow citizens prove their worthiness. This attitude has an enormously corrosive effect on society, leading people to wonder at each turn about the veracity of public statements and the sincerity of endeavors by others, and to waver in their own commitment to the public realm.

I hear people express their lost faith in politics and public life daily, and you will hear it, too, in the pages that follow. The current situation has left people openly struggling to know when something is believable and when they are being manipulated; when they should trust others enough to join together with them and when to go it alone; when they should be truly concerned about a public matter and when politicians or the news media are using an issue to pursue their own agendas. These questions dog people and give rise to self-doubt and mistrust.

My own work in communities suggests that when such doubts in one another are found in individuals, they experience great difficulty in making judgments that they feel are well informed, reasonable, and reliable; their personal confidence to engage in public matters suffers; their belief that others will join with them is eroded. Thus, the cultivation of the public's will for action — especially sustained action — becomes enormously difficult. Instead of the vibrant and robust public realm that I propose, we find conditions that stifle and stymie the process. But this is not the worst that can be said. There is another victim of this environment, an invisible one: when a semblance of reality is missing — when the pursuit of the truth does not seem to hold importance — then it is difficult to believe in what one sees or hears, and the trust in leaders, in various institutions, and in each other necessary to make politics and public life work disappears.

As I traveled the nation, I found that people trust few, if any, political leaders. Consider that statement for a moment; its truth is a damning commentary on the public life of American society. There is widespread complaint that public leaders too often focus on shallow matters, especially partisan and hot-button issues, and that they fail to talk forthrightly to the American people about their concerns. There is disgust among people that public officials reflexively turn to negative campaigning and rhetoric (though there is little doubt that such negative campaigning works from time to time), and this frustration is especially deep because political leaders seem so insensitive to the effects of such campaigns on the overall mood and health of the body politic. The common belief throughout the land is that public officials actively pursue their own interests at the expense of the common interest.

People say that these actions of public leaders routinely distort the concerns of ordinary people and fail to reflect accurately the reality in which ordinary people live. These beliefs are so strong and so deeply ingrained in people's hearts and minds that they make for an unreceptive, if not hostile, environment for any public leader who wishes to take a different path.

Equally sharp criticism is reserved for the news media, which people see as dangerous purveyors of distortion in politics and public life. Some people point to examples of good news media and in various of my own projects over the years, some of which were conducted for news media organizations seeking to strengthen their own credibility, I have found that people do see trustworthy news media outlets across the information horizon. But let me be clear: the sheer force of negativity in people's statements about the news media is overwhelming.

People are likely to say that the news media fail to cover important concerns, choosing instead to sensationalize and hype the trivial with an unfailing focus on the negative. Thus, people reject any and all notions that the selection of dominant news stories represents any approximation of the reality of their own lives or the life of the nation. The news media, they assert, make their choices based on profits, ratings, and personal agendas, rather than on the fulfillment of their purpose to inform society. Using much the same terms they apply to public officials, people say that the tone and coverage of the daily news leads to distortions in their sense of reality, diminishing what is important. Here, again, the result of these actions is to make people feel isolated, uncertain, and filled with anxiety.

You will see that people's concerns about political leaders and the news media did not appreciably change over the time period of the studies I report on in this book. You will hear other relatively consistent themes throughout these conversations. What did change, however, was how people felt in response to these concerns. Initially, amid people's anger, there was hope that such conditions might change. But over the years there was an unraveling of that hope, which contributed to people's retreat from politics and public life. We were to see this hope for change ignited once after the September 11th attacks. But that glimmer was soon extinguished.

The dilemma that people confront can be best summed up in this way. The very leaders and institutions they depend upon to help them make sense of the changing world are seen as playing with reality for their own gain. This creates a powerful emotion within people, one that alternates between anger and resignation, and one that ultimately leads people to feel trapped and powerless. People yearn to have their deepest concerns addressed, even simply acknowledged. Instead, their concerns seem to be routinely pushed aside and manipulated — all toward what end?

There cannot be engagement in politics and public life without some modicum of trust.

A QUESTION OF VALUES

There has always been a tendency in American society to boil down people's concerns and aspirations into a single phrase or slogan

— a mere couple of words. Perhaps it is a reflection of the influence of Madison Avenue or maybe it is simply part of the human condition.

Either way, during this time period, one of the exemplar phrases often touted as a synthesis of widespread concern came from the 1992 presidential campaign — "It's the economy, stupid." The line has repeatedly emerged in almost every election since the '92 race, serving as a kind of religious touchstone to guide candidates and their crusades. But the phrase, while perhaps a useful campaign slogan to rally the troops, is fundamentally inadequate when it comes to capturing the full essence of people's underlying concerns and aspirations.

Some pundits and pollsters thought that they had figured out this essence at the close of the 2004 presidential election. During around-the-clock postmortems, they dissected exit polls that suggested that one of the most important issues to voters was "moral values," a huge surprise to everyone who had bought into the conventional wisdom that the war in Iraq, the war against terrorism, and/or the economy were the central issues. During one television program made up of a panel of well-known journalists, a *New York Times* reporter suggested that "moral values" was, in fact, the big story she had missed during the entire campaign.

As I sat there watching the program, I wondered aloud: "How can that be?" How could a journalist covering the campaign miss such a big story? On second thought, it seemed not only possible, but probable. Many of us missed the essence of people's underlying concerns throughout the whole campaign — which is what makes missing the "values story" so important. Throughout the 15 years discussed in the following chapters, people have been in a near constant struggle with the notion of values — their own values, your values, *our* values. They ask, what do values mean? Who needs to hold them? How can we share them, especially as the nation becomes more diverse and fast-paced? Yet, for many observers, the story simply slipped by, often replaced by a narrative of acrimony and division, such as red states vs. blue states.

Actually, the wide concern about values was not lost on everyone. It was quite aptly discerned by a variety of political consultants, candidates, interest groups, and others whose daily business is not just to understand but, more centrally, to shape public opinion. To win political battles, many of these people made it their daily business to distort and sometimes manipulate the concern over values, using it to turn public opinion against political opponents.

You probably recall some of the heated "moral values" debates that have transpired over these 15 or so years. Many focused on various hot-button issues intended to tap into people's fears and frustrations. Remember, for example, the tumultuous debates over "family values" or "welfare reform" or, more recently, "patriotism." Recall, too, those skirmishes that have made use of various political figures — such as Hillary Rodham Clinton or Strom Thurmond or Jesse Helms — as the equivalent of human ink blot tests to ignite battles over values. Often these values wars were promoted by one political group or another to further its own political gain; sometimes they were used simply as a fund-raising tactic.

In a pluralistic society such as ours, heated debates have always been part of the political process, and it seems to me that they ought to be. But efforts to help people across the country sort out and address their growing dilemmas seemed noticeably absent during these "debates." Instead, they were notorious for engendering name-calling and demonizing people on various sides, and for their ruthless politics of personal destruction, presented as if they accurately reflected wide-spread concerns keeping people awake at night, as if they were some kind of genuine public service.

I have sat with people for hours on end and heard them talk time and again about the values-related concerns that make them feel unsettled. The issues discussed in the politically motivated values debates that dominated public affairs during these years were, by and large, not those concerns.

When you read these pages, listen carefully and you will hear people discuss the values that do concern them, values that genuinely stir their emotions, values that are in direct opposition to those embedded in the big "values debates." For instance, you will hear people ask how *truth* and *forthrightness* can find a more prominent place in politics and public life. They will speak about how people must exercise greater *loyalty* and *trust* between and among their neighbors and fellow Americans. You will hear people wrestling with the meaning of *community* and how to balance it with the desire for *individual control* in society. Notions of *social fairness* and *personal responsibility*, and how to define and restore them, are threads that run throughout all of the conversations. The desire for *these* values can be heard universally from people throughout the nation; they sit just beneath people's concerns and aspirations. Listening to these people, you cannot tell if they are Republicans or Democrats, if they attend church or not, and you cannot determine the region of the nation from which they hail.

People want to hold these values along with other time-honored American values, ones that we often hear a great deal about, namely those of *competition, individualism, and freedom.* These values, too, are part of the American fabric. But people believe that when they are pursued without sensible boundaries or limits, they can produce the materialism and greed, especially among individual citizens, along with the unscrupulous push for news ratings and vote tallies that now mark American life, and distort its goodness.

The conversations about values make me think that too many of us have lost sight of the values people seek to hold in common, values that contribute to people identifying themselves as Americans, values that make up the fabric of this nation. Instead, we use values to divide and manipulate and to set one group against another. The honest discussion of values will not by itself guarantee easy agreements on specific policy issues; such issues need to be worked out. But a clear recognition of the values common to many Americans can help produce a good society — one in which people, together, can reach for their own potential and work for the public good. Without this discussion, too many of us will go our own ways, pursuing our own individual needs, without concern for the public good.

IN SEARCH OF UNSUNG HEROES

People see everyday Americans as the antidote to the politics and public life they now experience. In the conversations from which I draw in the coming pages, people turned, time and again, to the role of the individual as the critical force to make right the course of the nation. What came through in these conversations, and comes through, I hope, in the comments I have selected, is the sense that people believe they hold a personal responsibility to participate in politics and public life. They believe that they are obligated to make good on the values they argue should find greater prominence in the public arena, but which have momentarily been distorted or escaped us. But when Americans look out over the nation, they see too many people who have turned inward, too many leaders and custodians of the public trust who have turned wayward. They believe that this dynamic must change. Now, as more than one person said, "You are either part of the problem or part of the solution."

Who will call people to bring about the change they desire?

What is clear is that people are waiting for someone to step forward to serve as the catalyst to get things moving in the right direction and demonstrate that change is possible. In some cases, they see as their role model individuals they call "unsung heroes" or "everyday heroes." Here, people do not have in mind the names of acclaimed individuals who have been lauded for some superhuman effort or selected for high position. Rather, they refer more generally to men and women who, when facing a challenge, have found ways to summon the enduring qualities of honesty, perseverance, and helping others. It is such unsung heroes and the fellow Americans who embody these values who will hold the credibility and trust to call people forward.

Whoever leads the charge, people suggest that change must emerge from small local efforts. A strong intuition exists among people that significant changes in society must begin in this way, bubbling up from the grassroots, one action building upon the next. People want these actions to be close to home so that they can experience the results first hand — to know that they are real. Indeed, people want individuals in their communities, or from nearby, to guide such efforts — individuals who they believe would understand their concerns and be good stewards of their communities. This is not an argument about Federalism; it is a matter of trust.

But, for now, despite any beliefs or desires that they should step forward, many people have found themselves struggling with what they could do to make a difference. They cannot see ways to enter politics and public life. After many years of being bystanders and spectators in public affairs, their imagination deserts them; they are left with few ideas and even fewer identifiable pathways.

THE REALIGNED RELATIONSHIP

There have been moments that demonstrate America's potential to do better. Immediately following the attacks of September 11, 2001, many political leaders, news media, and citizens altered their behavior, sending a signal of hope that out of tragedy some lasting civic-minded change might emerge. But, now we know that 9/11 did not change our politics and public life for the better.

There is a possibility that the public's involvement in the 2004 presidential election signals better days to come, inspired to some degree by new applications of the Internet. But such efforts might just as quickly fizzle out, as did the efforts engendered by Ross Perot's candidacy and the subsequent attempts to organize United We Stand chapters in communities across the nation. Let us hope they amount to something more.

What is clear is that the American people have been experiencing a long-term downward journey in their relationship with politics and public life. As you read these pages, you will find that:

- In 1990, people were expressing *anger* primarily about the state of politics. People felt pushed out of politics by self-serving politicians, sensational news media, and powerful special interests. Recall that this was the time when people turned to blunt instruments in an effort to regain control of politics, including the candidacy of Ross Perot, balanced budget amendments, and term limits.

- In 1992, people started to express what might be called a *felt-unknown* — an inkling that something they could not yet fully articulate was fundamentally off in the nation. People continued to be angry about politics, but they were becoming more worried that the political system was not up to the challenges of addressing their growing concerns.

- In 1995, people's anger and felt-unknown had given way to a fundamentally different emotion: there was a *deep lament* among people that the nation had not made progress on their concerns which, by now, they could more clearly define. The frustration with politics persisted, although people had begun to express the growing belief that individuals must play a more active role in the political process.

- In 1998, people had not seen any improvement in the condition of politics and public life, and they made the following decision: the only course of action was to *retreat* into close-knit circles of families and friends. This measure would enable them to gain some semblance of control over their changing lives and remove themselves from the disdainful world of politics and public life. Still, there was a growing chorus that the individual must step forward to create the change people seek.

- In 2003, people witnessed the vast display of patriotism that followed September 11th, but they became, over time, deeply frustrated that it offered a *false start* to repairing the nation's politics and public life. Thus, people made the decision to retreat even farther. Meanwhile, they said they were looking for "everyday heroes" to help change the course of their communities and the nation.

My sense is that people believe in their hearts that politics and public life is intended to work *for* them. Their views echo the sentiment expressed some 140 years ago by Abraham Lincoln in his Gettysburg Address… that "government is of, by and for the people." His mere 272 words still hold relevance for people today.

Lincoln spoke that solemn day of the "great task" before the nation, making reference to the challenge of self-government that the nation would need to meet. In the years following his landmark speech, the nation demonstrated that it could repair the breech left by civil war. The voices contained in these pages present a less daunting challenge, but still a fundamental one: what happens if people retreat from the public square, and too many of those who remain seek only to fulfill their own narrow interests?

Today, we must find the means to enliven politics and public life — so that individuals can tap their potential to make a difference in society and can join together to build a common future. The goal must be more than simply to solve immediate problems. It must be to create a good society, one that reflects people's best instincts and values.

Now, let us listen.

THE PEOPLE'S RETREAT

THREE

Pushed Out

THE TIME IS 1990-1991

Each day the proclamations by political pundits, newscasters, pollsters, scholars, and others grow louder. Their soundings are unmistakable. They say that the health of politics in America is at risk — perhaps even in rapid decline. Among the refrains the following two sound loudly: Americans are apathetic — they simply no longer care; and civic duty in America is dead or waning seriously — people do not participate in public life and politics.

Certainly there is much to lament about the country's public life. Participation in voting is low, and seems to be moving lower with each election. People's frustration about politics is high. Citizens lack a sense of political efficacy. And people seem to believe that the political system is often incapable of resolving major issues A good example is the debacle over the federal budget deficit, late in the 1980s, where politically charged debates persisted from year to year, political rhetoric became overheated, and dire warnings abounded — with little accomplished.

The sheer anger that citizens harbor about politics is seen at every turn on Main Street, America. The results of the 1990 primary elections show many signs of it. Incumbents are denied their party endorsement, political office-seekers who espouse populist rhetoric and positions are widely supported, and newcomers are sometimes chosen over establishment candidates. In the general elections, California voters pass referenda that limit the number of terms that state legislators can serve, and slash their staff budgets. "Throw the bums out," seems to be the mood of the day.

Yet, in listening to fellow Americans talk about public affairs, we find that many of the basic assumptions made by observers during this time are badly *misframed*. Discussions about politics and the public often focus on "voting" and how to make it easier for people to vote, rather than considering why people increasingly choose to stay away from the polls. There seems to be the belief that merely removing the influence of money from electoral campaigns will lessen people's frustration with politics per se, while failing to consider that the public may be yearning for something more in politics and public life than just clean campaigns. There are assumptions that what people need is *more* information in order to make political choices, when the issue may be that they need different kinds of information. I remember thinking during 1990 that we seldom make adequate time to look beneath the apparent symptoms of our problems to find out what drives them. We seek simple labels and equally simple solutions for our political ills.

What do the people say?

THE CONVERSATIONS

We conducted this first set of conversations in the middle of 1990 in six cities in six states — Dallas, TX; Des Moines, IA; Los Angeles, CA; Philadelphia, PA; Richmond, VA; and Seattle, WA. The conversations took place as the collapse of communism in the Soviet Union signaled the end of the Cold War. Earlier in the year, indictments had been handed down in the case of the Exxon-Valdez, which spilled more than 20 million gallons of oil off the coast of Alaska. "Apathy" was the buzzword of choice among political observers to describe the American electorate.

The conversations were sponsored by the Kettering Foundation, a nonprofit research foundation interested in the health of democracy. The purpose of the conversations was to explore such areas as: What do people think of politics today? What do people want out of politics?

How, if at all, are people involved in politics — and why or why not? What might be done to improve politics in America today?

We delayed the release of the findings from the first six conversations because of the Persian Gulf crisis, at the end of 1990. We wondered whether the war had affected people's views on the questions we had asked. So, in 1991, after the Gulf War, we decided to conduct four additional discussions — in Boston, MA; Denver, CO; Indianapolis, IN; and Memphis, TN — to gauge the potential impact. We found virtually no effect.

NO SEAT AT THE TABLE

I start with the dominant feeling underlying these conversations — the feeling of people that politics has been taken away from them, that they have been *pushed out* of the political process.

Having access to the political process is fundamental to our democracy. The idea that people have this access is often taken for granted. So long as the airwaves and newspapers are overloaded with information on policy issues, town hall bulletin boards overflow with notices of public hearings, and public officials scurry from one public event to another, we not only assume but loudly proclaim that citizens enjoy tremendous access to our political process. But this is not what we hear.

A woman in Philadelphia asks, "How long can you keep trying to be heard? You try to be, and you lose hard and then see that nothing will ever change." In Seattle, a woman remarks, "People say 'let someone else take care of it' because they don't think that they are going to be heard."

We hear many people like a woman in Richmond who comments that "years ago, politics was different. You could talk to your politician … Today politics is so big that it has distanced him from you." In Des Moines, a man goes so far as to say, "Public officials want to keep us away from them, because they don't want to hear us."

People want to participate, but they believe that there is no room for them in the political process they now know. "I'm never aware of an opportunity to go somewhere and express my opinion and have someone hear what I have to say," says a Dallas woman, adding, "I don't have time to sit down and write a letter. I don't even know where I would send it. I could write to the editorial page, but I wonder if anyone who is in a position to make changes would read it." A Des Moines woman notes that "I have been to too many public meetings wondering if I'm wasting my time." Her concerns are echoed by a Philadelphia woman who asks, "If people don't think they can have an effect, then why go?" The practice of politics during this period is such that citizens no longer feel just discouraged; they believe that they are actually denied access to politics.

This sense of impotence differs greatly from the so-called "citizen apathy" we routinely read about in weekly magazines and hear about on nightly news programs. Apathy suggests the making of a voluntary, intentional choice; most Americans feel, instead, that the current political situation has been thrust upon them. It is not something that they have chosen — or would have chosen — for themselves. A man in Seattle notes that "people do care very much, but they can't see how they can do anything about changing things."

This feeling of impotence appears widespread, and it seems to transcend sundry facets of how we conduct politics in this nation. It is revealed, for instance, in a fervent belief among Americans that individual citizens can no longer be heard on important public issues and that many, if not most, public issues are talked about by policy and opinion leaders, the news media, and others in ways that neither connect with the concerns of citizens nor make any sense to them. "People just don't have a sense of having valuable input to give," says one Los Angeles woman.

The feeling of impotence is also revealed in the belief of citizens that they have been squeezed out of politics by a "system" dangerously spiraling beyond their control, a system made up of lobbyists, political action committees, special interest organizations, and the media. In Richmond, a man mentions that "everyone in the state of Virginia is against drilling for oil in Chesapeake Bay. But just because every man, woman, and child doesn't want the drilling and Exxon does, you can bet your life there will be drilling. This makes me feel helpless."

LEAVING PEOPLE'S CONCERNS OUT

Virtually everyone in these group discussions expresses dismay over the particular issues that receive the greatest amount of attention today. Why? Because people seem to feel little connection to those issues; often, they believe that the issues are irrelevant to their lives.

A Seattle man says, "Politics is so remote...not involved with our daily lives." This is a common refrain. "I think our priorities are wrong," exclaims a Philadelphia woman. In the same discussion, a participant asks, "Do you feel that you have a say in where your federal tax dollars are going?" The group's answer is a resounding "no!"

These comments highlight the recurring theme that the issues talked about today, those that receive the most attention by the news media, political figures, pundits, and others, do not reflect the true concerns of most Americans. In one group after another, people say that the issues they are most concerned about — they frequently mention the issues of education, health care, roads, and the defense budget — often do not seem to rise to the top of the political agenda and rarely receive the kind of attention and action that they believe the issues warrant.

In Dallas, a man talks angrily about the need for increased prison space, saying, "In the end, the things we really need — like more prisons — are not being done." With other respondents nodding in agreement, he goes on to explain that Americans desperately want criminals put behind bars and that taking such action, at least in Texas, is a top priority among citizens. Yet every time government officials raise taxes, the priorities they set for how to spend those public dollars seldom reflect the views and needs of citizens. Instead of building new prisons, the officials spend the increased revenues on their own set of priorities. This man feels that such actions occur even when public officials "sell" the tax increases to the public as a way to pay for those priorities "pushed" by citizens.

A Des Moines man echoes this concern, if in a slightly different way. "It's hard for me to comprehend why they make big issues out of certain things, and other issues they don't care about." And a Dallas woman adds, "The issues that policymakers jump on the bandwagon and carry on about aren't really the issues that deal with mainstream people." At this point and time Americans feel that they have lost control over the political agenda — their concerns simply do not make it onto the docket of debate or, at other times, rise to the forefront of public discussion. At issue is not whether citizens, and only citizens, know what is important. At issue is that citizens in city after city, state after state, do not sense that their concerns are adequately reflected in current political debate. *That* is inimical to healthy politics.

People appear to be searching for a clearer sense of where they fit into various policy issues — of how the issues relate to them. As one Philadelphia woman puts it when referring to public meetings, "If bigger issues were localized — homelessness, education — then people would come out." A Richmond man says succinctly that,, "A lot of people don't see how they are affected." Citizens *want* to know not only how they are affected by issues but also why particular issues are important to them. No one seems to be helping citizens make these connections.

This concern is reflected in many group discussions. In Des Moines, for example, when talking about the federal budget deficit, one man states that he wants to know fundamental things about the issue before he can think about why action should be taken and what needs to be done. "How does it affect me — my life?" he asks. A woman then picks up the theme: "How is the pie divided up?" Another participant suggests that the deficit issue needs to be framed with the following questions in mind: "How much debt are we in? Where does the money go? What are the trade-offs?" He also adds, "What questions do we citizens have that we want answered?"

Many Americans complain that all the jargon, statistics, and other forms of "professional speak" used by public officials, the news media, scholars, and others can make discussions of policy issues difficult to sort out and comprehend. "There is so much the public doesn't understand," laments a Des Moines man. Citizens feel that without understanding the issues before them, they have little to offer to the public debate. When talking about issues and her ability and "willingness to think about them," a Seattle woman states, "I need immediate accessibility." And the views of many of the Americans in our group discussions are captured when a Des Moines woman, referring to elected officials and the news media, exclaims, "If only they would speak our language! You don't want to say that you don't understand, but people *don't* understand." A Richmond man uses some of the same words to make a related point. "Policy makers are speaking a different language," he says. "It's one of avoidance; it's one of 'it needs further study' — something that doesn't mean anything. They can have all of these debates on television, but when the policymaker is finished talking, you still don't know where he stands." The result of this problem, respondents say, is to push citizens away from participating in the political process.

The nasty tone of some political exchanges also keeps people out of the public arena. One woman in Des Moines laments that "in a recent debate, I hoped that the candidates would say something that would be really clear. But it turned out to be mudslinging at the other candidate. I feel like *making* them answer the question."

CAN YOU HEAR ME NOW?

There is no doubt that Americans yearn for open, public discussions among themselves and between themselves and public officials. "When you hear what others have to say, your views tend to broaden," says a Richmond man about the virtue of public discussions. A participant from Philadelphia remarks, "It's absolutely important that politicians hold discussions." He continues, "It's hard to ignore someone who is sitting right in front of you. You have to hear them." And a Seattle man, who described himself as being loathe to attend public meetings, says he would attend if public officials were more likely to listen to the views of citizens: "It would be nice to have a politician come in and ask us what we want as opposed to coming in and telling us, 'This is what I want to offer you.'" Indeed, a Philadelphia woman exclaims, "It would be ideal just to have a forum that is a discussion."

Many Americans now say that current methods for expressing their views, like hearings and public opinion surveys, provide them with neither the opportunity to learn about issues nor the forum to voice their concerns. A Des Moines man compares these methods to "whistling in the wind," and expresses doubt that public officials would listen to a group of citizens who held a discussion on an issue. Further, many citizens now suggest that they are at a loss about how to partici- pate in the political process — beyond merely pulling a voting booth lever every year or so. Without access to the political process, it seems certain that Americans will continue to feel disconnected from politics — they will continue to feel politically impotent.

To be clear: Americans believe that the problem with politics at present is not just that citizens do not have access to the political process, but that politics has been taken away from them.

THE SOUND OF MONEY AND POLITICS AS USUAL

To our discussion participants, the signs of this hostile takeover — seen today, perhaps, more than ever before — include legislative chambers overrun by lobbyists, air-waves filled with negative adver- tising, and news stories comprised of personal scandals about our leaders and their families. When a Philadelphia man asserts, "The special interests are in Washington 365 days a year. They have no trouble getting the ear of the congressmen or senators," his fellow par- ticipants nod in agreement. "Unless a politician feels threatened by the voting public," says a Seattle man, "they will go to a lobbyist."

Americans now feel powerless next to the mighty power brokers who, they say, govern politics. "How powerful is my one little vote if a PAC gave my representative $300,000?," asks a woman from Des Moines. A Philadelphia man asks the same question a different way: "Do you think your congressman is going to listen to you or someone who puts $10,000 to $15,000 into his war chest?" A Seattle man suggests that the influence of these power brokers has skewed the political process. "The whole process is corrupt — it's not issue oriented." And a man from Philadelphia remarks that, "Everything is special interests." A Seattle woman finds a small glimmer of hope. "Politicians are interested in how we feel about the issues," she says, but concludes that "they are more swayed by lobbyists."

Faced with this situation, many Americans throw up their hands and ask, "What can I do?" They feel that special interest groups, political action committees, lobbyists, and others have taken over politics; that these groups pursue their own agendas relentlessly — at any cost; that they cannot be controlled. In the end, citizens believe that they do not — cannot — have a say in this system. They do not have the raw power necessary to effect change; they do not have the necessary strength to make their voices heard. As one Seattle man tells it, "Citizens are part of a quiet group that doesn't seem to be noticed." A man in Des Moines puts this sentiment in more dire terms, saying, "They don't care about the people anymore."

WHAT'S WRONG WITH THE SYSTEM? EVERYTHING!

All the hoopla, speeches, money, propaganda, and sundry other aspects of political campaigns lead Americans to one fundamental thought, which a Richmond man puts this way: "Questions do come out of campaigns ... people begin to ask: 'What's wrong with our system?'" The answer, according to group participants, is virtually everything. On this score, Americans' concerns about political campaigns are no secret: there is too much money and mudslinging, too few good people involved in politics today. "You always have negative images [today] of people running for office," notes one Richmond man. A Des Moines man, reflecting back on the 1988 presidential campaign, suggests, "You can get into and out of office on a single [negative] issue ... case in point: Willie Horton."

Perhaps the most devastating outcome of the current state of affairs is that Americans want no part of political campaigns. Many are questioning why they vote; others simply have stopped voting. Even more troubling is the fact that most people would never entertain the notion of running for public office. "Sometimes they dig things up about candidates and it's just not right.... The result is that good people don't run for office anymore," a Dallas woman remarks. A Des Moines woman laments, "I want a candidate I can trust. But who is that today?" And a Dallas man suggests why finding trustworthy politicians is so difficult: "Many men have gone to Congress and then not sought re-election because they are disenchanted with the power brokers and the situation in Washington. It is not conducive to retaining the best people. They realize that they are totally ineffective, and they don't play that game."

The Americans with whom we talk believe the game of politics all too often results in nothing more than a lot of expensive posturing and cheap talk by those at the center of politics, those who control — or who seek to control — the game. "You get discouraged. Nothing materializes; they talk about issues but nothing happens. You hear them talk about the homeless; but nothing is happening," notes a woman from Richmond. People say they are turned off from politics by the inaction that they perceive. A man from Dallas observes that, "People get impatient with the lack of progress."

All of the bantering, arguing, accusing, name calling, and other antics that make up our politics have just become empty words to most Americans. Citizens believe that the dominant actors in our politics today create an environment where they all pursue *their individual* interests and agendas with little regard for the *common* good. Sometimes one or another actor succeeds outright in meeting a desired end; other times, several key actors must compromise among themselves. Citizens believe that larger needs — public needs — inevitably go unmet.

THE NEWS MEDIA: SOUND BITES AND NEGATIVITY

Americans believe that news media coverage of politics and policy issues leads to a sense of frustration and dismay among citizens. They say that this coverage pushes them farther away from rather than bringing them closer to participating in the public realm. It often does not resonate with citizens' concerns and the realities of life they experience and see around them. The participants in our discussions want the news media to promote informed political debate more actively. A Philadelphia woman laments, "The issues which get trumped up in the press, I don't care about. But I guess that's what sells newspapers. The healthcare problems, the homeless problem … all are diluted by this. These issues don't get the press."

According to group participants, the reporting on politics and policy issues is now driven by sound bites and negativism. Some citizens suggest that as the result of this coverage, Americans no longer care about their need to learn about policy issues. One Los Angeles man says, "The whole idea of sound bites getting a message across in 20 seconds — is absurd. Unfortunately, this is how most people learn about the events of the world." Group participants express regret not only about how this approach affects their ability to learn about issues, but also how it forces public officials to interact with the public. "Politicians have to couch things in such a way that the media can understand them. Everything has to be brief and quotable," maintains a man from Seattle.

This emphasis on conveying short quick pieces of information appears to have disconnected Americans from the substance of politics. One man from Richmond puts it this way: "The technology of the media and communications controls [politics]. It's sound bites, it's fast, it's quick. It has distanced every one of us from what's really going on, and has distanced all our political leaders from what's really going on with us, to a tremendous degree."

Group participants also believe that all too often the coverage of politics and policy issues is hampered by the negative spin that the media give to it. Scouring the streets for personal scandals, badgering some people on aspects of their personal lives, playing up arguments over small points between campaigners and among officeholders is the kind of coverage that troubles the American people. As one Philadelphia man says, "So much negativism comes out in the media about politicians that some people figure, 'What's the use?'" And a Los Angeles man suggests, "We think the way we do about politics because of all the negativism in the media and newspapers. We begin not to care."

In Dallas, a man cites the important role that the news media play in our society, "I think we need a public interest developed in order for people to participate. And maybe this is where our news media should come in."

POLITICS THAT GOES
BY ANOTHER NAME

Some observers might conclude from all of this that there is either little that can be done to ameliorate our political ailments or that the public is in need of some sort of shock therapy to resuscitate its political health. Fortunately, neither conclusion would be correct. We find that beneath the troubled view of politics expressed in our groups during this time is an American public that cares deeply about public life. On Main Street, America, we have discovered a strong — albeit often hard to find — foundation for building healthy democratic practices and renewed habits of public participation in politics.

Thus, with the avalanche of negative talk about politics in America, there also should be hope. We find citizens participating in various facets of public life in a political way, but they themselves do not naturally think of their activities as politics. Americans are willing to, and do, engage in activities that have inherently political qualities: they define the problems before them, set common purposes for action, and make choices for moving ahead. We find, though, that this isn't what they think of when they are asked about their political involvement.

In our discussions, it basically took just one question to lead to a positive discussion about public life: "How are you involved in your community?" Initially, people are stunned by this question, and hesitate in their response. They would ask, "Who, me? How am I involved?" It's not a question they often think about in connection with politics. Eventually, someone would come forth. A man from Des Moines mentions that he helped organize a neighborhood watch program. A participant from Dallas talks about being active in his local block association. Another Des Moines man remarks, "I've been involved in schools — on parent advisory boards." A man from Seattle reports that people there are "working on getting the city to preserve open space." Another Seattle resident says that citizens are "organizing to take care of public parks." In each of the groups, people note their work with low-income children, environmental groups, community-improvement organizations, and many other efforts.

Once started, citizens talk openly and forcefully about their community involvement. As these discussions unfold, it becomes apparent that those very individuals who had said that they participate in politics in only a limited way, *if at all*, in fact participate vigorously in numerous facets of public life in their communities.

With these examples before us, it seems clear that political participation emerges when some simple but powerful conditions are present, all of which seem to revolve around the notion of possibility: the possibility of having a say, the possibility of creating and seeing change, the possibility of fostering a sense of belonging within one's community, and the possibility of seeing and acting on one's own interest in an issue. These conditions (perhaps along with others) form what seems to be a compact between citizens and public life that suggests the following: when citizens participate, there must be at least the *possibility* to bring about and witness change.

Beyond this implicit compact lies a critical unstated element that determines how Americans view politics and public life at this time. Citizens believe that they must play a central role in any effort to reinvigorate politics; therefore, they disparage those who want to take the easy way out by pointing fingers at politicians, the news media, special interest organizations, and others as the sole culprits of our problems. They see the problem in a broader context — from which they do not exempt themselves. They recognize that they need to develop a richer understanding of policy issues in order to participate in political debate, they acknowledge that public officials face political constraints and pressures that are beyond their control, and they realize that they must work to have their voices heard.

Indeed, as a Richmond man says, "If we say we're frustrated and not going to do anything about it, then we won't. But if we keep trying, we might make a difference." A Des Moines woman puts the dilemma this way: "In general, the public is not very active in politics. It's like a snowball effect — you don't feel that you can have a voice; therefore, you don't participate, and you get farther and farther apart from your representative. Maybe if more people were active, our representatives would be better off."

As discussions progress, inevitably people would turn, on their own, to the importance of individuals thinking about and discussing policy issues. One participant from Richmond says, "I stay educated on issues." Others remark that they "talk to other people about issues." In Philadelphia, a participant states, "We hold afternoon coffees for 10 or 15 people in our homes to talk about issues." Another participant in that group remarks that "We have town meetings on local issues." In Los Angeles, we hear from a woman who organizes monthly breakfasts with speakers on policy issues. These comments always emerge as unrelated to the discussion of "politics." Indeed, when people are initally asked how they participate in "politics," such comments are seldom heard.

People do not consider their community involvement to be a part of politics. Nor do they consider themselves either involved in politics or to be politically efficacious. A Des Moines woman wonders, "Are political problems solvable?" before she decides that, "They're too big." The difference that emerges in our discussions is that people believe that community problems can be acted upon by people working together, but that political problems, according to these citizens, cannot. "Community involvement brings about change," says one Dallas man, "politics doesn't."

To the people in these conversations, "politics" occurs in a place they do not see and is done by people whom they do not know. "When I think of politics, I think of Washington, not here," says a Dallas woman. In Des Moines, a woman observes, "What we do locally isn't perceived as being part of politics. It's because we perceive a personal connection locally that we don't perceive when you move beyond this level." As one Seattle woman puts it, "We typically think of politicians when we think of politics — not community activities."

People also separate their community involvement from politics on a more fundamental level: politics is dirty, messy, bureaucratic, and the domain of professional operatives. It is the extreme opposite of what they seek through their involvement in the community. "Politics is rules, laws, and policies. This has nothing to do with why I am involved in my community," notes a Los Angeles woman.

Significantly, the discussions on politics and community involvement are, in effect, reflections of each other. As citizens talk about their community involvement, they describe in positive terms the presence of characteristics whose absence they deplore in the political process. At the community level, they say, it is possible to be heard and valued in public debate, it is possible to help bring about change, and it is possible to feel a sense of efficacy in managing and improving public affairs.

A few see the connection. One Dallas man comments, "Community involvement should be considered politics, but it's not." A Los Angeles man goes so far as to say that community involvement "is political in a truer way. It's people organizing to make things better. That's what politics really is."

WHAT ABOUT THE GULF WAR?

As we prepare to release this study in 1990, the Persian Gulf crisis has emerged. We decide to wait until the war subsides to conduct more citizen discussions to check our findings. We want to know whether the war in any way changes how Americans view politics.

We hold the first two additional conversations in March 1991, in Memphis and Denver, during a period of two days when the news media — print, radio, and television — are providing extensive coverage of returning American soldiers and prisoners of war from the Persian Gulf. We ask the same set of questions as we did in the original conversations. Each group starts with the question, "What do you think of politics today?"

In Memphis, the response is unmistakable — and immediate. Four people around the table reel off one-word responses one after another: "Sorry"... "Crooked"... "Political"... "Unbelievable." The Denver discussion takes a similar direction, with participants saying: "It's lost the interest of people." "Gets really old." "A lot of special interests, too many special interests... We don't have any say in it." From the time of this first question until near the end of the two-hour discussion, the responses we hear echo those recorded in the conversations some six months earlier. The Memphis and Denver participants mention the Persian Gulf War only in passing.

Not until the end of each session, when the moderator raises the war specifically as a topic of discussion, do people talk at any length about recent events in the Persian Gulf. The responses are clear: the war has had absolutely no effect on the participants' thinking about politics. These views emerge despite findings from various public opinion surveys at the time of rising patriotism among Americans and increasing citizen confidence in the government. Indeed, President George H.W. Bush is enjoying his highest approval ratings ever — often hovering at or over 90 percent. One participant even says, "Patriotism has gone up dramatically, but I don't think that has anything to do with political issues."

Two more groups are held in Boston and Indianapolis in May, and these discussions echo the observations made in the initial discussions as well as in the Memphis and Denver sessions.

In these discussions, we find that apathy is not rampant among citizens. A sense of civic duty is not dead. Americans are not indifferent to public debate and the challenges our nation faces. Americans simply want to participate in the process of representative government. They are angry and frustrated — they feel pushed out — but the possibility exists that they again will engage with public life at both the national and local levels. A Seattle woman describes the climate as one in which "People have gotten so disappointed that they don't want to get involved anymore. Yet, there are a lot of people who still want to act."

And we see that they do act in the immediate world around them. Despite the anger and frustration that people passionately express when they discuss politics, they find comfort participating in what they almost do not recognize as the political lives of their communities. The belief in the power of community, together with the concrete actions that people are taking on behalf of their communities, offer hope that a deeper public participation in politics can be encouraged.

FOUR

Rising Anxiety

THE YEAR IS 1992

S ome two years ago, the nation celebrated its quick and decisive victory in the Persian Gulf War. President George H.W. Bush's approval ratings were sky high; people's self-described confidence in government was, too. Now the spoils of victory are a faded memory, giving way to more anxious times.

Earlier this year, the nation watched in horror as Los Angeles erupted in riots following the acquittal of police officers charged with the beating of Rodney King. In August, consumers will rejoice when the Mall of America, the largest shopping mall in the nation, opens in Minnesota. A few months later, the tagline "It's the economy, stupid!" will come to dominate the political landscape in the presidential race. It is a phrase that makes for good political sloganeering, but it fails to reflect adequately the true complexity of people's concerns.

People's frustration is not merely about the persistence of politics as usual, a focus of our discussions in 1990. Nor is it solely about the nation's current high unemployment numbers, for statistics alone cannot offer an adequate measure of people's concerns. No doubt, people are concerned about jobs — in particular, their *own* jobs. But their sense of discontent and troubles runs much deeper. They speak of an American dream that is endangered and seemingly beyond their grasp.

There is the growing belief that individual expectations are running too high in the nation, with materialism and greed becoming the accepted norm. Many wonder if people are still willing to make sacrifices for the common good. In this America, trust is a scarce commodity — trust in politics and political leaders, trust in the news media, trust in economic and government institutions, trust in one another. People are feeling increasingly isolated from one another. They believe that the rules that govern society are being twisted and turned and redefined.

This is not the America people seek.

All this turmoil leads me to think about a new kind of "misery index." The traditional misery index, you may recall, takes into account inflation and unemployment and was a hot topic of discussion during the days of President Gerald R. Ford, when it received constant attention during his fight to whip inflation. Today, in the year 1992, a redesigned index might focus on people's discontent concerning bedrock values. Such an index would cast a broader, more foreboding shadow than the traditional statistical measures could ever express.

There are a variety of concerns in the mix of discontent today — politics and leadership, the economy and people's fading economic dreams, social values and the role of community, to name the most easily visible. Each factor raises the level of people's frustration; taken together, they give rise to enormous feelings of anxiety and uncertainty.

A cautionary note: The intensity of people's unease may offer a dangerously misleading impression that they are more ready for change than is the case.

THE CONVERSATIONS

These conversations were undertaken just as the nation was gearing up for a presidential election that saw the upstart candidacy of Ross Perot and the eventual defeat of President Bush, the incumbent, by Bill Clinton.

Knight Ridder Newspapers asked my colleagues and me to conduct conversations across the nation in seven communities with Knight Ridder newspapers. The aim was to provide insights both to inform the news organization's 1992 election coverage and to frame a CNN-

Knight Ridder nationally televised Town Hall special to be aired from Wichita, Kansas.

The conversations focused on such questions as: Who were people's heroes growing up? What about today? How would people describe the American dream to someone from another country? To what extent do people think government is capable of acting on the challenges they see in the country today? Under what conditions, if any, would people consider making personal sacrifices for the nation? How do people see politics today?

We talked with people in the seven communities of Columbia, SC; Detroit, MI; Philadelphia, PA; St. Paul, MN; San Jose, CA; Tallahassee, FL; and Wichita, KS. In four of the communities, the participants consisted of people from a single generation — the Depression generation (ages 68-91), the Silent generation (ages 50-67), the Baby Boom generation (ages 32-49), and the Baby Bust generation (ages 18-31) — chosen to reflect a cross section of the nation in terms of education, income, party affiliation, and race. In three communities, the participants consisted of an equal number of representatives of each generation.

THE FELT UNKNOWN

The anger people expressed two years ago in 1990 about the condition of American politics and public life has given way to something less focused but no less bitter: a powerful unease and anxiety about the state of the Union. Now, America finds itself mired in a conundrum. While there seems to be a general, fledgling consensus among people about what is wrong in the nation — the government isn't doing its job, the news media aren't doing their job, citizens aren't doing their job, and a variety of specific issues seems to be bubbling up — this consensus is best characterized as tenuous and unfocused.

One might compare this situation to what happens when people who are facing a dilemma together experience difficulty in figuring it out. It is not uncommon in such situations for someone to yell out to other members of the group: "Don't just stand there, do something!"

A similar sentiment can be found throughout the nation at this time. People are anxious and want to alleviate their unease. As one Tallahassee man put it: "There are too many people saying [the nation is] going down hill, it's going down hill! If you think it's going down hill, propose something to make it work. Do something about it!"

Perhaps, then, the most accurate way to characterize the state of America today is to say that people are experiencing what might be called a "felt unknown." Isaiah Berlin, the philosopher, describes this feeling as the sense within someone that something significant is amiss — that there is an inkling that something is off — but the individual is unable to piece together and articulate the whole picture in an integrated fashion, to name it for what it is. This is not a comfortable feeling, obviously. It is a feeling that prompts anxiety.

To the extent that Americans are experiencing a "felt unknown," the inability to name the problem at hand poses a significant challenge for Americans, their politics, and their leaders. After all, naming a problem is an essential step to understanding what needs to be done to resolve it and to assuming responsibility for taking action. With an unnamed problem, it becomes inherently difficult to *know* what is at issue and to decide how to deal with it. This situation leaves people in search of a sense of coherence about both their lives and the nation.

In the spring of 1992, while people feel an urge to move ahead, they wait, unclear about how to pursue the very change they hope for.

THE GOVERNMENT THAT ISN'T THERE

You can hear an uncomfortable sense of anxiety in people's discussions about government and public leaders. No doubt, people want to have faith in the public sector; after all, they want their most pressing concerns to be addressed. But so much of what people see swirling around them leads them to be mistrustful and frustrated. Their misgivings are echoes of our 1990 conversations, only the misgivings are more pervasive and more deeply felt. One St. Paul man reflects a common frustration when he says, "It seems like when you leave it in the federal politicians' hands, it gets to be: 'I'll take care of mine... and everybody else can go by the wayside.' I just don't have that much confidence in politicians anymore." And a Philadelphia woman claims that the government is "Everywhere else but here where we need them."

Part of the story is the widespread belief that government is wasteful, spending people's hard-earned dollars on unnecessary items. Throughout the 1980s, Americans heard the constant drumbeat about government "waste, fraud, and abuse." This was part of Ronald Reagan's platform, not to mention the battle cry of many other individuals who sought to lead government or influence policy and public discourse. Such discussions continue today, as when a Philadelphia man suggests, "We have to stop the government spending $500 for a hammer," referring to news media accounts of waste and fraud in the Department of Defense and other departments, where such items as a toilet seat, which can be purchased inexpensively at a local store, become exorbitantly expensive. "We have to go into each department and clean it up," the man proclaimed. Many people express doubts that the government can prevent such waste, given its sheer size and scope. One San Jose woman puts it this way, "Government looks like a big jellyfish. It's an enormous, huge thing." She and others wonder how you can give shape to this behemoth.

One result of these sentiments is that people now sound as if they are all natives of Missouri, the "show-me state." They seem to be saying: "*Show me* government can be different!" And only if they are given adequate evidence will they be willing to step forward and support government action on their concerns. A Tallahassee woman says that she wants a specific plan from leaders who propose new spending: "Show me proof," she demands. "Show me proof of what you're going to do." In the same spirit, a St. Paul man suggests that people would be willing to consider making sacrifices if they could see the right actions being taken, "I think that most Americans, if they got the right kind of leadership, would be willing to sacrifice a lot if we could get ourselves out of debt."

But the right kind of political leadership seems woefully absent today. "I think there's no dynamic person right now running for any office, nobody to look up to," laments a Philadelphia man, adding, "We are in a lot of trouble." The lack of inspiring new faces on the public scene offers people little hope that progress will be made on their concerns. *This* reality led many people in these conversations to say that they would need to settle for the status quo. A Tallahassee man notes: "I think politics is always going to be politics. I'm not sure it will change."

But change — at least a certain kind of change — is what people want. One Tallahassee woman alludes to the change people seek when she talks about a new attitude among voters. For some time, she says, voters seemed to be more concerned with a candidate's appearance than their vision or stand on issues. Now, she observes, given the changes in the country, the tide is turning. "What people want now is someone to deal with specific issues." Another woman in the same group agrees with the need for such change, though she has yet to see it. "They're missing the important issues," she says. "They're going for cosmetic values rather than what really matters in society."

Almost uniformly people believe that government could act effectively on their concerns if government officials were to change their orientation. For one thing, they need to focus on more than just what benefits them. For another, they need to put the emphasis on long-term solutions. People are tired and suspicious of the pursuit of the quick fix. They also argue that priorities must reflect the 1990s, as opposed to replaying over and over again the arguments and topics of the previous decade. Today, people say, there needs to be less emphasis on defense and international affairs, and greater attention to domestic concerns, including education, health care, and the environment.

THE DESTRUCTIVE MEDIA

A continuing theme from our conversations two years ago is people's sense of frustration with the news media. If there is any change since then, it is that as people's anxiety about their own personal affairs and the affairs of the nation increases, their views of the news media only worsen. As we shall see, this dynamic will widen and deepen in the years ahead.

People feel flooded by negative messages from the news media, stories, they say, that are counterproductive to understanding the issues and challenges before them and to remaining hopeful about the future. They are particularly concerned about personal attacks. A St. Paul man suggests, "Don't you think the media is responsible for a lot of the negative things? The first thing they do is try to dig up all the dirt about anybody who comes into the public eye."

A Tallahassee man sums up his frustration with the media by saying, "The reason people have such bad opinions about the politicians is that the main things that get sensationalized by the media is the dirt ... It's not the platforms, it's not what they stand for that everyone knows about." Voices such as this tell us that the negative focus of the news media can nullify the steps that some political leaders take to connect with citizens in a meaningful way.

A Philadelphia woman says of the news media, "They tell us everything we don't have to know on TV and in the newspaper. They're not being honest, and that's why we don't, half the time, know what's going on." In one conversation after another, there is a pervasive sense among people that print and television journalists are not telling people the whole story. This perception — no, this *belief* — not only engenders a lack of trust in the news media, but it also adds to a feeling among people of being manipulated and a sense of not being in control of their lives.

Perhaps there is nothing worse than feeling anxious and being in the dark.

IS THE AMERICAN DREAM DISAPPEARING — OR JUST CHANGING?

A government and news media you can't trust. Clearly, this eats away at a person's confidence. You can see some of its effects in assorted unhappy views about the status of the American dream.

To many people, the American dream seems to be disappearing. They once believed that if they got a good education and worked hard, they could succeed in America. Today, they question that fundamental belief. Now, people assert that it is more who you know than what you know that helps get you ahead. They see employers who discard employees as if they were disposable and interchangeable. They witness economic institutions such as savings and loans collapsing around them. People have deep and pervasive concerns about the national debt, their jobs, the ability to support their families.

Across the country, there is growing concern that economic opportunities are shrinking as individuals and their families struggle to make ends meet. People are wondering whether there is the opportunity any longer for them to pursue the American dream, or whether it is merely a memory of the past. Listen to how this San Jose woman talks about the American dream: "I was raised with [the belief], 'If you work hard, if you get educated, you'll get a great job.' That doesn't necessarily hold true. You have to have a chance."

A *chance* — that is what is at issue. People's diminishing sense of possibility crosses all generational and geographical boundaries in these discussions. A Philadelphia man who grew up during the Depression gives voice to the confusion among people who feel that the promise of America has been broken. "You worked all your life to have something and all of sudden you have nothing. And what happened?" Attempting to answer his own question, he responded softly, "I don't know."

A Tallahassee woman describes her mother's notion of the American dream this way: "When my mother came to this country, she was a nursing student married to an American serviceman. To her, the American dream was to go to America and set up her home; educate her children and learn about this country; and know as much as she can to be a contributing member of society and her church." For her daughter now, this dream seems out of reach and perhaps on interminable hold.

Amid all the talk about the American dream, there is a persistent undercurrent of frustration among people that they will not be able to make any progress on their larger concerns about the nation so long as they remain on an economic treadmill. Their economic concerns demand too much of them, particularly since they are unsure about what they need to do to regain a sense of economic stability and a sense of control in their lives. According to one St. Paul woman, "I think people feel like they are drowning and grasping for straws. I think the harder you work, you're not getting anywhere." A Tallahassee woman, referring to some people's desire to do more in their community, states it is simply not a viable option under current conditions. "We're trying just to stay alive," she observes. "We want to do more, but the way we are now, we're barely surviving."

An accompanying view of many people is that the American dream is being slowly turned into a vivid nightmare as a result of people's obsession with consumption and materialism, a perspective that did not appear in the 1990 conversations. A man in Detroit claims, "We have pursued materialism and all the goodies that come along with it too strenuously as part of the American dream over the past 40 years. That's why we're seeing the ruination of the country today." For this gentleman, and other people in these discussion groups, the American dream was once about sharing in a larger vision of America. Now, it is about hoarding more and more material goods.

Many people see such materialism as part of a larger phenomenon — the distortion of the American dream by unfettered individual pursuits that have undermined its meaning. But some see this expression of individualism in a more neutral way, "The American dream still exists, but it's individualized," says one Tallahassee man. He frames the American dream now as people's own individual pursuit of freedom and money and education — whatever they seek.

These conversations on the American dream often find their way to the issue of *individual* opportunity. A Wichita man says that the American dream is "the opportunity to do what you want." This, he says, is a reason for celebration. "I don't think that a lot of people in other countries have the opportunity to do what they really want." Another man in Wichita adds that the American dream is "the opportunity to realize what authority is in a democracy, and recognize that, and do whatever you want to do." He also asserts that, "The American dream is just as much alive today as it ever was."

For some people yes; for others, not clear.

WILL PEOPLE ACT FOR THE GOOD OF THE COMMUNITY?

That so many people do not believe their concerns are being adequately addressed by those in leadership positions only compounds their anxiety about the course of American society. They express deep doubts about whether they and their fellow Americans will hold at bay their allegiances to their own narrow interests long enough to give time for the common good to form and emerge. A woman from Tallahassee seems to be imploring anyone who would listen when she says: "We should become a 'we'-oriented society instead of a 'me'-oriented society and we could get something done."

For many people, American culture is too driven these days by materialism, greed, and self-centeredness. They say that expectations for personal gain run too high and that social values of respect for others, working together, and the common good are often missing.

Many people believe that the good of the community should be the concern of each and every citizen, as evidenced by the St. Paul man who says, "That's the American way; I think we all feel that we should be involved in the welfare of other people — our neighbors and people who aren't as well off as we are." People believe that they must play a larger role in solving problems in society. But people are ill-prepared to act — in terms of their knowledge, their wallet, and their frame of mind. Most participants are uncertain about how they would go about securing their own individual welfare, let alone focus on improving the welfare of others.

In most of these discussions, participants argue that people need to reset their expectations about material gain, increase their sense of community responsibility, and reduce their pursuit of greed. But taking action on these desires is another matter altogether. Throughout these conversations, people make clear that they will step forward *only if* they are certain others will join with them. And so, absent any common engagement on the challenges before the nation, a kind of conspiracy of silence seems to set in. It is as if there is an unspoken agreement among people that "if you don't call me out" — that is, if people are not confronted in a serious way — "then I won't say anything to you either." As one Philadelphia woman says, "The attitude is that people want to take care of themselves first today." And a San Jose man observes, "We feel powerless to do anything."

There is another factor that needs to be weighed in considering the likelihood of whether people can act together in pursuit of the public good. Listen to this Tallahassee woman who claims that not only do people not know their neighbors but that "they're afraid of them."

Afraid? Yes, of their neighbors, a changing economy, politicians and news media who distort their reality. This fear leads some people to withdraw from others, in an effort to gain some sense of control.

The notion of retreat is not a predominant theme in this set of conversations, but it nonetheless seems more prevalent than in the conversations of 1990. A San Jose woman describes her retreat in this way, "I'm starting now to make changes in my life and do things that are much more personally inner-directed ... I'm really working hard, perhaps brainwashing my daughters . . . being aware of who they are as women and that's the most important thing."

There can be no common good if there is no commons.

SACRIFICE IS FOR SUCKERS

Given their distrustful views of the government and the news media, and their sense that they are on their own, what do people think of the willingness of Americans to make sacrifices for the public good? Not surprisingly, people predict that it will be nearly impossible, partly because, in their experiences, they cannot trust politics and the "political system" to distribute sacrifice fairly. Indeed, sacrifice is for suckers. People ask, "Will others pay their fair share?" "Will I get stuck with the bill?"

The lack of trust is not the only barrier. There is also significant unease among people about how much value younger generations place on notions of sacrifice. Many people wonder aloud about whether younger people will honor existing social compacts such as Social Security when their time comes to pay. Some people see younger generations as too impatient and too demanding. As a Philadelphia man puts it, "I think during Depression times people were more appreciative of what they had... the young expect everything all in one day."

Other participants suggest that younger generations are not appreciative enough of what previous generations have sacrificed in order that they can enjoy the benefits of a good life. Many participants even complain about their own children. A St. Paul woman observes, "We want to give our children what we didn't have. But maybe we forgot to remind them what we had to give up to give them what we have." Some people go so far as to claim that the current disregard for sacrifice has led to greediness within younger generations. Another woman from St. Paul, a member of the so-called silent generation of the 1950s, adds, "I think my generation learned to live with less. Our children want to live with more."

Given all the emphasis on individualism and materialism in the nation, many people have lost hope that their fellow Americans will make a positive impact in politics and public life. "People [once] seemed to be out for helping each other," laments one Tallahassee woman. "Now everyone is into themselves and wanting to just get what they can get." A few discussion participants show some willingness to consider paying more in taxes, if that were necessary. But almost always, there are strings attached. "I'll pay my fair share if someone else does," says a St. Paul woman. Here, again, people are in search of proof they will not be out on a limb by themselves. Little faith exists in the ability to take a step forward and not get ripped off.

The desire for people to pay their "fair share" — and to show proof of participation — extends in an interesting way to political leaders, too. Some people tell us that the only way they would agree to make sacrifices is if public leaders directly shared in the pain. Public officials should take pay cuts or reductions in staff and pursue some other financial measures — all in the hope that these would serve as demonstrations of acts of good faith. This notion of a public demonstration of shared sacrifice — that everyone is participating and no one can outmaneuver the system to escape responsibility — runs deep in these conversations. One Tallahassee woman puts it this way: "The politicians don't need to make as much money as they do. Why don't we invest that money into fixing up these places, to create places for people to live?" If sacrifices are to be made, people want politicians to ante up.

How likely is this to happen? Most participants see public leaders looking out for themselves rather than for the people they serve. A harsh assessment comes from a Philadelphia man: "The politicians sure try to make improvements so they can really enjoy themselves ... they're feathering their own nest and filling up their own pockets."

LOCAL ACTIONS, LOCAL HEROES, STEP BY STEP

But there is another, more positive side to all of this.

Consider the comments of a San Jose man: "I'm an American citizen, so I'm part of the solution or I'm part of the problem ... you can't be in limbo. So you make the commitment to vote, get involved in some civic organization." This sentiment of civic responsibility, if you will, clearly exists within people, notwithstanding the fact that it can be difficult to activate today. It is possible to hear from one conversation to the next, coupled with people's frustration, even resignation, that they do not know how to act upon it.

As in 1990, what is certain from these conversations is that people believe that public-spirited action is necessary and that it must start locally and must be taken in small steps. People envision a change process that unfolds through a host of little actions that eventually collect into a force to improve conditions in America. Through this work people believe that they and their fellow Americans will rediscover how to join and work together — and eventually scale up their efforts.

According to one San Jose man, Washington D.C., as well as some state capitals, is too far removed from many of the problems people face, "The people in their local areas can handle local problems a lot better than a big government." Local folks are more likely to understand people's concerns; people also can have a more intimate connection with local officials working on their behalf.

Here is how one Tallahassee woman explains this course of action. "Small things have to happen," she says, "If we start working together on little things, we can get together on bigger things." It is from small steps that people develop faith in their own capacities. Only then can collective action emerge. According to some participants, as people take small steps, change can begin to flourish and the country can be redirected. A man in Tallahassee notes, "You got to start at home, in your own backyard before you can get your country on the right track."

A Wichita woman explains, "With so many people trying in little spots here and there across the country, I think it shows that it can make a difference — the ordinary, unsung hero or people without famous names or famous reputations can really make a difference in our country."

While heroes have held a special place in every culture from the dawn of time, in these conversations, people are thinking of neither gods nor celebrities when they spoke of heroes. Instead of individuals with superhuman prowess, people are looking for heroes with whom they can personally identify, women and men who are more believable and fill roles that are more attainable for ordinary people.

One man in San Jose defines a hero as an individual who decides to take action, making this observation: "Is a hero someone who is an ordinary person but lives up to heroic aspects in a difficult situation? I think so ... So I think that most heroes are someone that continues to do the right thing, even if it's not an easy time."

Increasingly, Americans are turning to people who are making a difference in day-to-day life as heroes — people who demonstrate qualities of personal perseverance, helping others, honesty, and other admirable traits. While some people named well-known political or entertainment figures as heroes, others are in search for something more authentic — the unsung heroes who genuinely improve their communities in their own matter-of-fact, down-to-earth ways.

WHEN THE CONVERSATIONS ENDED...

Ordinarily, when a group conversation is over, people simply stand up to begin their journey home. But in these conversations they were to remain in their seats talking to their fellow group participants, sometimes for up to 40 minutes or more. They stay and wrestle with the issues and concerns they had placed on the table; they seem to reach out even more to those with whom they had just shared their thoughts and personal stories. To many people who observe these conversations, this dynamic is striking, if not a bit of a paradox. Over the course of the conversations, the participants seem noticeably depressed by their discussion, even withdrawn at times; yet they are visibly grateful for the opportunity to voice their concerns and hopes and, yes, their fears — their fears about America, their communities, and their families. In each group, it feels as though this conversation might have been the first meaningful opportunity for participants to talk with people other than those who are close to them; to piece together and begin to make sense of their common concerns.

If a public meeting were called for the Americans taking part in these conversations, who would show up? Based on these discussions, people likely will first ask: "Who else might go? Should I go and take the risk that I'll be the only one there? Can anything good emerge from such efforts?" People wrestle with what role they ought to play.

These conversations often lead participants back to the topic of their own responsibilities in politics and public life. On the one hand, they assert that they need to be "heroes" in their own lives, for themselves and others. They do not see government necessarily coming to their aid, so they must act. "All of us have capabilities to help their fellow man. That's what we need to do as individuals. I don't believe it's [only] government's business," notes one Tallahassee man.

On the other hand, this reality cannot be escaped: Even though people hold out admiration for every day heroes, they do not necessarily know what to do or how they can make a difference in their communities. They feel bombarded by images of negativity and materialism in the news media. They are told everyday how to be consumers, but nary a word is spoken about being citizens. This barrage leaves people feeling discontented with their situation and worried. They do not see the tools they need to help them break out of their cycles of frustration. While wrestling with this reality one Tallahassee man emotionally states, "I would say that there are issues that are on people's minds now [that] are not coffee-table talk, that they are gut-wrenching issues that really make us lie in bed, wide awake, and stare at the ceiling, and wonder about what we are leaving for our children. And what we are building for ourselves."

The challenge in America is how to create a path forward for people even as they feel such anxiety about the state of the union and their own futures. There is the nagging sense that something is amiss in the land, but it has yet to crystallize in people's minds or in a common language. This sense of a felt unknown, this prevailing uncertainly, so far serves only to fuel people's anxiety.

It also makes it difficult to take action, especially if there is a need for people to make any kind of sacrifice. People believe that ordinary

Americans will get stuck with the bill and that government will waste their hard-earned dollars. They are afraid of being "ripped off" by political leaders who pursue their own interests at their expense. They believe that their fellow Americans — the neighbors that some even fear — will not join with them.

One Philadelphia woman describes how her lack of faith in government prevents her from sacrificing. "I guess I'm just selfish. I don't want to give anything that I worked for and have now in order for the government to tell me that this is what they're going to do."

The anxiety that many people feel about their own economic situation and the nation as a whole makes the decision to step into the public square highly problematic. For some, it seems they are waiting to be asked; others seem to want permission. Either way, they are looking for someone they trust to call them forward in an authentic manner.

A San Jose man expresses the need for citizens to take ownership over what he sees as a broken system. "There's no honesty in politics anymore. So I believe that individuals, citizens of the United States, ought to be actively involved ... so these things don't happen."

For now, however, people are not prepared to step forward. They wait, anxiously.

FIVE

The Struggle Within

THE YEAR IS 1995

In April of this year, the nation is rocked by the terrorist bombing of the Murrah Federal Building in Oklahoma City, which leaves 168 people dead. Throughout the year, President Clinton battles with the Republican Congress led by Newt Gingrich, resulting in a shutdown of the federal government in November. The 1996 election cycle approaches.

Today, citizens' views of the Union are significantly different from the outlooks expressed in the conversations of both 1990, when Americans lashed out at the "political system" with anger, and 1992, when people experienced an inkling that something larger was amiss in the nation but were unable to place a finger on the exact cause. Today, the tone is one of lament, not anger or simply anxiety. We find people in a more reflective and introspective mood — sad that more progress has not been made on their concerns, increasingly fearful that the nation is losing a sense of humanity.

Today, people see with great clarity two fundamental — and inextricably linked — challenges before the nation.

First, they describe an economy that has turned into a kind of quicksand, which is slowly pulling some Americans under and fast endangering others. The emergent economic rules of today's society seem to them to be grossly unfair — from how corporations treat their employees, to who shoulders the burden of taxes and budget sacrifices, to the growing gap between the incomes of the rich and everyone else.

Second, they express a great fear about the disintegration of social ties, families, and values. As adults are confronting tougher economic and personal demands, neighbors and communities are turning inward, and many people believe that too many children are being left to raise themselves. The result is a tremendous void — filled by faceless institutions, television and its messages of violence and hate, and society's infatuation with materialism.

What all this adds up to is that people are clear on a set of common concerns.

But this is only half the story. People do not believe that America has either the will or the capacity to tackle the tough questions that confound the nation. And so, as the 1996 election cycle approaches, people are in search of a new kind of leadership. They believe the nation must find this leadership not only among politicians but also within the news media, among citizens, and among all those concerned with the health of politics and public life. Most importantly, people are focused on the *conduct* of individuals and institutions, saying that the conduct of both must change if America is to set the right course for its future.

THE CONVERSATIONS

As my colleagues and I set out to capture the voices of citizens in a new set of conversations, the nation is riveted by the constant news coverage of the O.J. Simpson murder trial, a far cry from the concerns of our participants. The conversations have been commissioned by the Pew Center for Civic Journalism as part of its Citizens Election Project, an effort to demonstrate new ways of covering politics.

In all, we held 15 conversations in the fall of 1995, at the outset of the 1996 presidential cycle, to establish a reference point for journalists covering the campaign. The conversations are being held in four of the most hotly contested battleground states of the primary season — California (Los Angeles, Modesto, San Diego, and San Francisco), Florida (Jacksonville, Miami, Orlando, Tallahassee, and Tampa), Iowa (Davenport, Des Moines, and Mason City), and New Hampshire

(Claremont, Laconia, and Nashua).

The discussions focus on such questions as: How would people describe the "state of the union" today? What do they think about politics; and what do they want from politics today? What does it mean for sacrifices to be spread fairly and equitably within society? What is the role of the news media during an election year? What is the role of government, citizens, leaders, and other institutions in addressing people's concerns?

ECONOMIC QUICKSAND

A growing sense of betrayal marks people's outlook, based in part on the belief that the nation is splitting in two — with the wealthy getting wealthier, and the middle class getting poorer. People believe that they exercise little control over the future. They are disgruntled that a basic standard of fairness now seems *routinely* and *widely* violated. To many, the country they love is being ripped away from them.

"I have to work twice as hard to get by," is how a San Diego woman sums up her daily struggle to make ends meet in her life. People look around and see that the well-paying jobs they once held are now gone, supplanted by low-skill, low-paying, low-benefit positions. Economic opportunity and security are both slipping away, and their fears and frustrations about these changes are palpable.

In these discussion groups, people say repeatedly that the current economic situation prevents them and their fellow Americans from fulfilling their aspirations to work. A Jacksonville man asserts that people want to work but are experiencing enormous difficulty in finding the right job. "Put us back to work," he pleaded, "but not at McDonald's." Many Americans are finding it hard to keep their heads above water. "It is not easy to keep pace. It's just a day-to-day...struggle to survive," a Claremont woman says. For many individuals, it is one step forward and two steps back. At issue is not whether many people want to work, but if they can find a job that will adequately support their family. As for people who say they have made progress in this economy, they often feel as though they are in danger of losing their hard-won gains.

Articulating a more widespread concern than we heard in 1992, people are worried, even fearful, about their abilities to build better lives for themselves and their children.

People are quick to blame corporate leaders for these problems. They say that such leaders recklessly place too much emphasis on the pursuit of profits and in turn have upended the current economic rules of society. "Corporations had more of a social conscience at one time," laments a San Francisco man, "now it's just purely profit." Indeed, people complain bitterly that corporate objectives now focus solely on the bottom line. A Jacksonville man says, "Big business keeps trying to get fatter and fatter and fatter!"

Over and over in these discussions, people talk about how corporations simultaneously seek to increase both profits and layoffs, while at the same time cutting such worker benefits as health care. "A lot of companies — they cut back," notes a Jacksonville woman, "What do they hire?" She answers her own question: "Part-timers with no benefits."

People believe that in the past U.S. companies have always found ways to innovate as well as expand the economy, but current corporate practices make people wonder how America will build a world-class economy for the future. "You cannot develop as a nation without developing methods, new products, and technology in general," a Nashua man asserts. "I mean, you're gonna die eventually."

All these changes make people wonder what will come of the social compact — the implicit yet enduring agreement they once took for granted — between employees and workers. They want employers to exercise more loyalty to their employees *and* to America. They want business to reinvest in their plants and equipment and stop moving offshore. They want jobs with benefits — the kinds that will help people support their families. They worry, though, about whether such actions are possible in today's world — indeed, whether corporate America can exhibit a social conscience.

The economic squeeze that people feel is only made worse by a tax system that many see as inherently unfair. People are quick to assert that the middle class pays far more than its fair share of taxes, which only angers them as they run harder and harder just to keep up. But the tax issue hides an even deeper concern, one that strikes at the very heart of people's notion of America. Participants see a widening income gap between the very rich and everyone else in the nation. Listen to the comments of this Des Moines woman: "The difference...between what the guy in the field, or the guy in the production line, or the guy on the construction job, makes and what presidents of the companies make — millions and millions of dollars these people make. There is a great inequality there."

Her comments come as millions of people across the country have become more aware of excessive corporate executive salaries while workers lose jobs and withstand dramatic economic dislocation. The result deeply troubles people and gives rise to extraordinary feelings of betrayal. A Miami man observes: "You've only got two classes of people now — the very rich and the working class." A Mason City man says, "I'm starting to wonder if the American dream still exists."

ARE WE IN THIS TOGETHER?

As economic security seems to slip away from them, people see the bonds and fairness of American life slipping away too. Most of these concerns echo attitudes we heard expressed in the 1992 conversations. For example, while people say they are willing to pay their "fair share" to help others or invest in the nation, exactly what "fair share" means, who pays, and under what conditions, are all up for grabs. A Mason City woman illuminates this tension. "I don't think people mind paying their taxes if they know the rich are paying their fair share." And a Laconia man suggests, "People are willing to get to the point where I'll give up my program if everybody else gives up theirs."

People fundamentally feel that they have been "suckered" in years past, and they are deeply suspicious of any proposals that suggest "fair sacrifice." They reflexively ask, Will those with more resources ante up? Will less well-to-do Americans be stuck with the bill? Just what is fair sacrifice at a time when so many people feel that a sense of fairness has been so blatantly violated?

But there is a dimension to these conversations that did not appear in 1992. When can we expect people to step up and make the requisite effort to provide for themselves?

As an Orlando woman observes, "I have nothing against helping people, but let's not pay their way." And a Davenport man wrestles with this question when talking about people in need: "The homeless and the people who are starving, most of them need to help themselves. But that doesn't mean that we should be turning our backs completely...But, on the other hand, some of those people know how to use the [system]." People struggle with how society might help those individuals and families in need and not feel used themselves.

THE DISAPPEARING FAMILY AND NEW BABYSITTERS

Something has also happened to the American family.

Throughout these conversations, people describe America as a nation made up of parents stressed out by economic demands and too focused on their own personal needs, oftentimes leaving their children behind to rear themselves. Too many parents nowadays are missing from the daily routines of their children. "It's like the whole family structure isn't there anymore," says an Orlando woman. Another woman in the same conversation adds: "The mom and the dad that should be there with their kids...are too busy working two and three jobs to make ends meet." "The kids don't have a home anymore," one Des Moines man observes. And a Tallahassee man comments, "There is not support of the family around any more. Too many children are growing up without guidance."

People also worry that parents no longer have the support of the community as a safety net to help guide kids. Observes a Jacksonville woman, "Before, the family extended into the community. Now the community has shut the door and said, 'You take care of your own. I don't want to get into your business.'"

When challenged on why so many people have turned away from helping other families, discussion participants say that they are afraid to "get into" the business of being concerned about children around them — fearing that they will be accused of "abuse" or be chastised by a child's parents. They are fearful of being seen as busybodies, sticking their noses into someone else's business.

The African proverb, "It takes a whole village to raise a child," is mentioned in literally every discussion group. The sentiment seems deeply held among people from one community to the next. Maybe it goes without saying that everyone in a community needs to pitch in to raise children; indeed, people are quick to tell personal stories about how an adult other than their parents shaped their upbringing. But listen to this Orlando man, who, after making reference to the African proverb, says, "But we can't do that anymore...you could pull a child from in front of a moving vehicle and... you're going to get sued!" Most people in these discussions feel uncomfortable accepting this perspective, but they can not envision a way around it. At the same time, many would agree with the comment of this Laconia man: "It takes a community to raise a child, and that is probably more true today than it was."

Many participants say that instead of assuming their parental responsibilities, people have wrongly come to expect schools to be substitute parents. A Tampa woman complains, "Everyone feels it's the schools' responsibility to teach manners and good hygiene and sex and all of this." She adds, "They're just pushing it off on the schools." And an Orlando woman remarks, "Your kids are in schools and day care, and it's just like the whole family structure isn't there anymore."

Besides using schools and other places outside the home to raise their children, participants say that too many Americans are using television, movies, videos, and music to fill children's days and occupy their attention. A Davenport woman asks, "Aren't we as parents sometimes sitting that kid down in front of the TV just to get them out of our hair?" A Des Moines participant provides a blunt answer to that question. "Parents use the TV as a babysitter." Central to people's sense of frustration is their belief that they are losing control of their children. The impending result, according to one Miami woman, is that, "MTV is gonna rule your house!"

OUT OF CONTROL MATERIALISM

People are especially concerned about this trend because they see television and popular culture in general as undermining cherished American values. They report that much of popular culture is based on messages of consumption and materialism, which they believe contribute to social problems from crime to family breakdown to the lack of community. For many people, the focus on consumption and material-ism revolves around the desire to have it all – to get what you want, when you want it — without any sacrifice or obligation or patience. "Every-thing now — you don't wait for anything," a Modesto woman points out. A Tallahassee man says, "People are working all their time to buy this, buy that, for kids…and we're investing everything into material posses-sions. We're forgetting about what the foundation was."

According to many, the inability to satiate the desire for consump-tion leads people to want more than is necessary, or even more than they can afford. Everyone is striving to move up the economic and social ladder — but at what cost?

One Orlando woman frames the problem in this way, making a comparison one can often hear around the country: "We can't drive a Toyota putt-putt. We have to have a big Maxima. We have to be suc-cessful because of our mind-set, because we've been 'Americanized' to this pop culture." A Mason City woman sums up what many people in the group discussions are feeling when she points out that, "We got too materialistic. The nation. The family. Everybody." Participants view America's infatuation with materialism as a corrosive cancer spreading throughout the nation.

TAKING PERSONAL
RESPONSIBILITY

The primary treatment for reversing society's ailments regarding disintegrating families and values, according to group participants, is for each American to reassume — or assume for the first time — personal responsibility in her or his daily affairs. Many of the challenges people see come down to individual behavior — what people do in their daily lives. But they suggest that widespread changes in this area can evolve and emerge only through societal norms, and cannot be mandated by legislatures or edicts.

"The morality and family value thing...you can't govern those things. You can't legislate that," says a Des Moines woman. And a Modesto man adds, "It's not a governmental thing. I don't have to have a law...to tell me you must watch your neighbors' children or you will be fined." He notes that such responsibility belongs on a "personal level."

The importance that Americans place on the value of personal responsibility cannot be overemphasized, nor should it be diminished through simplistic and manipulative political rhetoric. Says a Laconia man, "We know what the golden rules are, and there are a lot of people in our society not playing by those rules." Yet people are not clear on how to take action to infuse these values into the public realm. "How do you get the common, average, everyday person to say 'I want to do something'?" asks a Tampa man.

All this discussion harkens back to the role of community, and people suggest that current trends cannot be reversed unless entire communities pull together to raise "their" children. As one Tallahassee woman notes, "To some extent, other people's children are your children. Responsibility for your society is your responsibility." But people wonder how that can happen now — who takes the first step?

And exactly what is the appropriate or desired role of government in this evolving context? On this question, as on many, people are not sure how to proceed. "I have mixed feelings about it," asserts a San Francisco man. "On the one hand, I want the government out of my business. On the other hand, I realize that there needs to be some amount of oversight or control to protect people." Or consider this comment from a Modesto man: "People want government off their backs, but they're afraid. They see kids who are carrying guns and becoming pregnant out of wedlock." When it comes to social service agencies, schools, child care centers, and other areas in which government might play a role, people are divided among themselves, and often within themselves.

And what of the news media?

"THEY'VE LOST WHAT THE TRUTH IS"

Thomas Jefferson wrote about the obligations and dangers of a free press in a democratic society. He, like so many keen observers of democracy, saw a pivotal role for the press in our nation's deliberations. But some 200 years later, after billions of dollars of investment in the establishment of the news media, the people tell us that they cannot rely on the fourth estate to help them understand the challenges that affect their lives and the nation. In short, people believe that the news media have lost their sense of the truth, and they complain bitterly that too often news media coverage lacks essential accuracy, failing to reflect how things really are.

Our participants spoke about this a good deal. If their views do not substantially differ from the views in earlier conversations, they are stated more frequently and with more force.

"It's more than just selling papers," remarks a San Francisco man on the purpose of the news media. "They have a moral responsibility to the people of the United States to write the truth and not just fiction." It is this sense of responsibility that people feel has been abrogated.

People want the news media to exercise more responsible judgment in their daily work. A good place to start, they believe, is to put greater emphasis on the substantive news that people need to know in order to make informed judgments. Pointing to an example of what she wanted, a Des Moines woman explains, "On C-SPAN they have the two sides on all the time." She adds, "And those people don't yell at each other." A Miami woman remarks that she is looking for "the negative and the positive together... Just balance both... Give the public a chance to choose." A Modesto man makes this plea: "Show a little discretion in what you're putting on."

Throughout these discussion groups, participants say that the news media twist and turn things, and in the process, their stories lose meaning and relevance. Listen to this Jacksonville man: "If you want to bring out some points about a specific person's character, bring them out as they are." But, he continues, "Don't turn them, don't twist them around. Don't tell me the man that walked on water couldn't swim."

Or consider this point by a woman in the same group. "If you're going to talk about what he did wrong, okay, talk about it. But give an accurate picture. Go ahead and give it exactly as it is and not... paint it to make it sensational for your newspaper."

If there is a bias that concerns people about the news media, it is not one of leaning politically left or right, but rather one of the media slanting their coverage toward notoriety. The result is places too much emphasis on some stories and misses others entirely. Group participants repeatedly say, as this Tampa man does, that they want the news media to "report the news, not make the news." People feel that in the news media's rush to put their own slant on news, they neglect stories that are important to society. A Jacksonville man suggests, "There's a lot of important news that they're ignoring." And another Jacksonville man accurately sums up the sentiments and frustrations of many people in the discussions. "They lost the idea of what they were there for," he concludes, "They've lost what the truth is."

Current news coverage makes many people throw up their hands in disgust and walk away from the news and thus a key source of needed information in politics and public life. "When it goes on and on and on, you just get so tired of hearing about it that you just don't care anymore," a Mason City woman notes. "I turn a lot of it off because I get sick of it," a Laconia woman remarks, "We're just over-saturated." Discussion participants believe that the news media cynically base their news decisions on profit motives. "They do it for the ratings," a Modesto woman argues. And a Davenport man agrees, "The media go for their [rating] system on whatever they do."

All in all, current news coverage overwhelms people's patience and sensibilities. "People get so burned out," a Davenport man says, "they don't want to watch anymore." Another Davenport man makes this damning observation about the lack of seriousness found in much of news coverage: "The way the media has covered the O.J. trial is the same way they cover politics." The result of such coverage, according to a Nashua man, is that "the media boils things right out of the water."

LOOKING FOR LEADERSHIP

At one point in each of the conversations, we ask participants if their public leaders are doing a better job of fulfilling their aspirations since the time of the 1992 elections. After all, just before the 1992 election, and since then, there has been quite an explosion in the use by public officials of town meetings, focus groups, fax polls, bus tours, and other means of gauging public attitudes and connecting with people. Ross Perot made these techniques a mainstay of his 1992 candidacy; Governor Bill Clinton made use of bus tours during his candidacy and is employing town hall meetings during his presidency.

After watching and sometimes participating in such initiatives, what do people think of them? Do they see these efforts as helping to bring about the kind of leadership they were in search of? Do they feel more connected with their leaders?

No sooner is the question asked, than the answer comes: "No!" Recent efforts by public officials have left people wholly *un*satisfied that their leaders are making genuine attempts to understand the concerns of citizens. Rather, they see these efforts as gimmicks that leaders use to gather reconnaissance on the public, only to apply the resulting insights to curry favor, to appear being responsive, even to find ways to manipulate people's emotions and positions. Consider this point by a Claremont woman: "Are they listening to us because they really care what we think about, or because they want our vote?"

The comment of a woman in Jacksonville seems a response: "They're listening, but they're not paying attention."

Many people argue that public officials use public opinion polling numbers merely to justify their own positions. Here is an Orlando man who is suspicious of efforts to listen to the public: "You could give me a poll and tell me how you wanted it answered. I could probably call the right people and get the answer just like you wanted."

People assert that their elected officials will do virtually anything to secure electoral victory. "[Politicians will] put their finger up and say, 'Okay, what's the latest poll?' The only thing they're concerned about is being re-elected," says a Davenport woman. And a woman from the same discussion group argues that during campaigns there are "no truths coming out." She goes on to say, "Everybody [is] worried about how they can damage their opponent instead of worrying about how they can actually do some good for people."

What one takes from these conversations is the sense that people believe their public leaders are engaged in a kind of game of charades, a game, they say, that continues as *they* struggle to make ends meet. A frustrated Davenport man notes, "We're busting our butts trying to make ends meet, and here these upper-income politicians are gloating around and more or less blowing hot air towards us." He continues, "People are just getting fed up with it."

At the core of people's concern remains the fundamental belief that many leaders simply do not understand how people live or the essence of their concerns. "They really don't get a broad-based understanding of where the people are at," a Nashua man observes. Another Nashua man suggests, "They don't have an understanding of real life anymore."

One Davenport woman says that if public officials did walk in the shoes of ordinary people, they would be better representatives. "If they could live [here], for one day, then they would understand where we're coming from. Because they've got bodyguards, they've got limousines, they've got fancy restaurants — they don't know what it's like in the real world. They live in *their* world." Regardless of whether or not all politicians have bodyguards, people believe their democratically elected representatives live in a world of their own — apart from them.

People want leaders who demonstrate vision and conviction. Instead, they feel bombarded by "hot button" public debates that make a mockery of their heartfelt concerns. Participants assert that single words or phrases — such as "family values" or "personal responsibility" — are used in politics to incite people, and often do. "They're trying to stir us up," complains one Los Angeles woman.

A Tallahassee man suggests that this kind of engagement makes him wonder exactly what public officials really care about. "We have no idea if this politician actually cares about the topic or is just using it." And another man in that group, speaking about hot-button debates, says: "It seems to have led to a rule by rhetoric — leadership by individuals who hate-monger, who push intolerance, who push social division as a political agenda." He then suggests that no one has a corner on this kind of conduct. "This happens...on both sides of the political spectrum."

The conclusion people draw from these experiences is clear. "The people who are going into politics are not for the people. They're for themselves," says a Jacksonville man. "They're there for the good life and the good pensions, and stuff like that." Indeed, people believe leaders are more in tune with the needs of moneyed interests than the people's interests. "In order to get involved in politics, in order to run for office, you have to be in a certain tax bracket," a Tampa woman believes. "You've got to be dealing with corporate America." This is the same corporate America, people say, that does not care about their future.

Ultimately, then, a potent emotion of betrayal by public leaders fills each of these conversations. "They say what we want to hear so that they can get elected, and then they do what they damn well please when they get in office," a Modesto man angrily suggests. People feel fooled and manipulated, entangled in a kind of open season of bait and switch. Each election, each time they hear a public official speak, people hope for the best; only too often they feel let down as they watch this bait-and-switch relationship unfold. Here is how a Miami man sums up the dynamic: "When we give them the OK, then they come up with something else, and they fool us." To a Los Angeles man, this situation means the following: "We're voting on one thing and getting another."

At the end of the day people ask their leaders relatively straight-forward questions: Do the leaders understand our concerns? Do they care? The answer, to discussion participants, is quite clear. As one Los Angeles woman puts it, "Nobody's interested in the good of the plain old public anymore." She and others argue that politics and public life are being driven by leaders who have become singularly obsessed with winning elections and pursuing personal gain; they have lost sight of their public responsibility. That responsibility, according to one San Diego woman, requires, at a minimum, having a genuine understanding of ordinary people. "Get back down to where the average person is," she says. "Get back to where everything starts." That will not be an easy chore for most politicians, according to these Americans.

PUBLIC LIFE: WHERE DO WE BEGIN?

"There's an old saying," a Modesto man recalls, "When you point a finger at somebody else, there's three more pointing right back at you." He continues, "A lot of the problem goes right back to the people. We like to sit and complain, but we don't do anything about it." People can see the fingers pointing back at them and deeply believe they must do something to right the wayward conditions of the nation.

"Everybody needs to get involved," says a Tampa woman. I don't think it's a case of where we can sit back and just let somebody else do it anymore." The notion that people must wrest control of the situation and direct more of the action in politics and public life can be heard throughout these conversations. A Des Moines man argues that people could have "so much more of the voice if we chose to be interested, so that the lobbyists would just be a little squeak." People assert that they must jump more directly into the political battle — into the work that needs to be done throughout the land. One Tallahassee woman notes, "You can't fight a battle from the outside."

If any progress is to be made, people say, they will need to start working together toward common goals. "People pulling together for a change instead of fighting each other" is how one Davenport woman put it when talking about the kind of involvement people must embrace. And a man from that group replies, "The public has to do something....We can't just sit here and talk about it and talk about it...and forget about it. You've got to take some action somewhere down the line." Taking such action will require people to alter their worldview; they can no longer be out just for themselves.

As one Jacksonville woman points out, "The responsibility has to start with [the] individual." An essential part of that responsibility is for Americans to become better informed so that they can participate more. This notion, of course, echoes the 1992 conversation concerning news media. "People don't make their own judgments all the time," a Tampa man says, suggesting that too often Americans merely accept at face value what they read or hear. And a Des Moines woman confesses, "It's my own fault for not going out and making an effort to find out who is for and against what." Over and over people observe that they need to make more time to read and listen and think about what is happening around them. What's wrong now, they suggest, is that too many people have their heads in the sand.

Of course, people say, if the nation is to correct its course, then more Americans must reassert their right and responsibility to vote. One Los Angeles man says of voting: "We're the big democracy. We're supposed to be voting, voting, voting." He continues, "These people are dying in other countries just for the sheer pleasure of voting, and we just sit there and say, 'Oh no, not today.'" People in these discussions assert that the ability to vote is a beloved privilege, and one that more people must exercise. Yet many people take a pass on voting, participants note — upwards of 90 percent in some local elections. Some people say it is because of the sense of futility that comes with even this brief engagement in public life.

Among all the suggestions for re-engaging people, maybe the most essential is for Americans to re-ignite their sense of belief in themselves. Despite the negative view often expressed about the nation, participants argue there is much for people to believe in. A Laconia woman, speaking about the sense of patriotism in America, says: "It's there, more than we can see." For the people in these discussion groups, patriotism is not an empty label. It refers to people's love of country, their respect for others, and their desire to pull together for the future.

A Nashua man comments, "People still like to help each other out." It is this basic sentiment and its corresponding actions that people seem in search of. People believe there is a wellspring of such sentiment waiting to be tapped within the country if the conditions are right. As one Davenport woman says, "There are people out there, trying to better things." An Orlando woman captures the tension that now exists in America and the difficulty of moving beyond it when she states, "People really do care, even when we say we don't."

Listening to these conversations leaves one with the distinct feeling that something basic is missing in America, an element that is fundamental to our collective understanding of ourselves and this nation. A San Francisco man puts his finger on what many people are concerned about. He says, quite succinctly, "We've lost our sense of humanity."

It is a Tampa man who notes that the nation is going through tremendous shifts and that people need time to sort through them. "Society is moving fast.... It's just coming right at you, and people are more reactive to it." He says about Americans, "They are trying to cope and deal with the absorption of it, and rationalize it, and say...'What's the right and the wrong thing?'" The answer, of course, is not readily apparent.

The very essence of humanity seems to be squeezed out of routine interactions in daily life. According to what our participants say, it is missing in people's interactions in their communities, with their children, with regard to politics, and in coverage by the news media. The sum total of these diminished interactions leaves Americans feeling that the country they love is disappearing — and that they are as responsible as anyone else. A Laconia man puts it this way: "We've lost our soul." People around the table nod in agreement.

One thing is certain: people are clear that money is not the answer. Perhaps not so surprisingly, this response comes at a time when consumerism and materialism seem to govern so much of people's lives. Indeed, participants say that the challenges associated with America's changing conditions cannot be fixed by government agencies merely upping budget allocations or by increased consumer spending. Nor can money satisfy the need for people to exercise greater personal responsibility, or for political leaders to be more authentic, or for the news coverage to reflect people's reality more accurately. Doubtless, money can help in some areas; but money is no substitute for basic personal engagement, effective ideas, and principle-based decision making. An Orlando man echoes the views of many people in the group discussions when he says, "Money's not the solution." Rather, he points out, "Changing the way they do things is the solution."

But where is such change to come from? And when?

It will come slowly, people say. They are sure to remind one another that it has taken years for the nation to find itself in its current state of affairs, and it will require time to alter its present course. "It's not an overnight thing," a Tampa woman notes. A Tampa man adds, "It takes a long time with a big ship." The United States is a very big ship indeed, and while people yearn for a new direction, they want to be realistic in how long it will take to set a different course.

Against these glimmers of hope, consider the comment of a Mason

City woman: "A lot of people say... 'I'm just one person. What difference am I going to make?'"

There is a struggle within America to discover the capacity and will to move in a new direction, and to be guided along the way by a renewed sense of humanity.

SIX

Closing Down

THE YEAR IS 1998

It is about a decade since I began to talk with Americans about the state of U. S. politics and public life and their relationship to it. Now, in 1998, my colleagues and I have been commissioned to learn how Americans define "civic renewal" — a term that has come into greater use in recent years by some working to strengthen public affairs in the country — and to explore what it means to them.

But that endeavor is not to be. We quickly see that the group participants can not talk about "civic renewal." Americans in these discussions almost uniformly say that the phrase rings hollow to them. As one man from Dallas explains, referring to those who regularly or routinely talk about civic renewal, "They come up with words to try to express ideas, and they want to make sure that those ideas, when people first hear them, are positive. But it's a lot of mumbo-jumbo — a lot of fluff, a lot of icing."

Instead, people in these conversations seek to talk about the state of America — the country, its people, themselves. The discussions do not have a "civic" tone to them — people do not talk about attending public meetings, or volunteering in their community, or about the need for some kind of collective action on a pressing public concern. They talk about "life" and how it is to be lived in America. The reports are dismaying.

These Americans tell us that they and their fellow citizens have *retreated* from American life — an act they abhor, but they see no other route to take at this juncture in American history. They have retreated because they see a nation in which the societal messages and values and behaviors do not square with the America they want. They believe the nation has lost its way; misplaced important values; and over-whelmed, at least temporarily, the place for basic human interaction guided by a sense of humanity. These Americans suggest that change must start, not with legislative fixes or grand schemes, but within the individual. Americans must pause and examine who they are and who we seek together to become.

THE CONVERSATIONS

It is a time of relative economic prosperity when we visited Dallas, TX; Denver, CO; Des Moines, IA; Los Angeles, CA; Memphis, TN; Philadel-phia, PA; Richmond, VA; and Seattle, WA for this set of conversations.

As we talk with people across the country, the news is dominated politically by an investigation into the conduct of President Bill Clinton, which leads to his impeachment in the U.S. House of Representatives. Abroad, coordinated bomb attacks on American embassies in Tanzania and Kenya kill 224 people. In response, the United States government launchs cruise missile attacks against targets in Afghanistan and the Sudan. Late in the year, former professional wrestler Jesse Ventura is elected Governor of Minnesota, and oil company, Exxon, acquires Mobil — creating Exxon-Mobil, the largest company in the world.

These conversations, commissioned by the Kettering Foundation, focus on questions that include: How do people see and experience America today — how would they describe it; what do they seek? What is the condition of politics and public life in the nation, and in people's communities? What will it take to create the kind of change people seek?

As I listen intently to these conversations, I am reminded of the enduring American credo implicitly consecrated at our nation's founding: that this is a nation always becoming. The people in these conversations are struggling in some fundamental way with the contemporary meaning of this American ideal. Maya Angelou's poem, "On the Pulse of Morning," speaks eloquently to the soundings of Americans today:

> *Today the Rock cries out to us, clearly, forcefully,*
> *Come you may stand upon my*
> *Back and face your distant destiny,*
> *But seek no haven in my shadow.*
> *I will give you no hiding place down here . . .*
>
> *The Rock cries out to us today, you stand on me,*
> *But do not hide your face.*

The voices we hear in America today come at a time when the nation is enjoying one of its longest periods of sustained economic growth. But these voices signal to us what Americans are still unsure of — their visions of the fundamental direction of the country and what is to become of America.

SEEKING COVER

Many Americans report that the people of this nation have never worked harder for longer hours than they do today, driven in part by the swift and powerful changes they are experiencing. These changes can be overwhelming, and, indeed, is so for many. And as people talk during the course of an evening, sitting elbow to elbow with perfect strangers, revealing moment after moment their thoughts, their beliefs, their fears and dreams, they ask just where that effort has brought this nation of ours.

As people, in effect, lift their noses from their daily grindstones and contemplate the America that ebbs and flows outside their own doors, they do not like what they see. Their response? Rather than striving to help change things, they lock themselves in their homes, working in order to live *apart from* the very society in which they want to find their place once more, which they hope to shape and guide, over which they would like to exert some control. A woman from Richmond expresses such sentiments in this way, "If you look at the whole picture of everything that is wrong, it is so overwhelming. You just retreat back and take care of what you know you can take care of — and you make it smaller, make it even down to just you . . . just you and your unit. You know you can take care of that."

She and others say that a driving idea of American society today, an idea that has captured their attention since they themselves were young — since so many of us were young — is "the bigger, the better!" But these folks now question this adage. They say that bigger is less personal, less connected, more out of control. What they see is not the America they seek. People said they want to regain a sense of control in their lives — and the only way they can envision today for achieving that goal is to create smaller comfort zones around themselves. "They want to stand in a shell, a comfort zone," a woman says in Denver. "People retreat," observes a man from Richmond, "because you have control."

Most people describe their comfort zones as close-knit circles that begin and end with families and friends. Some people in these conversations use such words as "clans" or "pods" to describe these groupings. In many of the conversations, people talk of "like going to like." But their expressions are generally not echoes of the woman from Philadelphia who, during one of our conversations, speaks about growing up in the Italian section of town, where people knew each other, where there was an enduring feeling of warmth and belonging; rather, this was more of a retreat into the smallest unit possible — to keep away everyone *other than the people to whom we feel directly or comfortably connected.*

Wanting to talk about *this* America comes quickly to folks; there is little hesitation in their words or voices. "These communities — it's a natural way that humans behave," says one Richmond man. "The wolves have packs, the whales have pods, fish have schools — almost everything in nature groups together in groups that are suitable to one another." In Los Angeles, we hear similar thoughts. "People like to live in clusters," says one man. People nod in agreement as such sentiments are expressed. Pulling back from the larger society around them seemed appropriate; more to the point, it becomes a form of self-protection.

Most people express the recognition that while they could, or should, do more to reach out to others, in fact they rarely venture outside of their immediate circle. A woman in Richmond puts it this way: "We should all do our part as far as helping others, but people have gotten to the point where they say, 'This is about all I can handle.'" A woman in Seattle explains: "It all goes back to family. We need to take care of our own family." And a Denver woman, whose comment is representative of her group, asserts: "I don't even really want to know what my neighbors are doing."

When one Seattle man looks out at America, this is what he sees: "hopelessness, a tremendous tension and confusion in our culture that is a fuse." He continues, "It's a fuse burning." Americans are seeking cover; they are retreating from the larger society around them.

OUT OF MANY, ONE?

American history is filled with notions that this is a nation made up of rugged individuals, of pilgrims and pioneers. But in this country's early years, individual efforts went into building a single nation. Our ancestors sought to create better lives in a land of opportunity: *E pluribus unum* — out of many, comes one.

But now people question if our much-heralded individual efforts are contributing to building the nation, or if the efforts are so narrowly focused that they simply lead only to personal benefits. In our conversations, people assert that far too many Americans, including themselves at times, have turned inward, and are now focused so intently on themselves that they leave little room for others. They question if a nation can function in this way. Says one woman from Des Moines, "I would like to have the hope, but I don't see anything is going to change. I see people where I work and who I associate with — and they have dreams and goals for themselves, but they don't have dreams and goals for the country."

As we talk with people in communities across the nation, the very notion of what it means to be an American today troubles many. "Our future is deteriorating because we live in a country of hyphens; there are no more *Americans*," says a man in Philadelphia. He then continues, seemingly yearning for a response from someone: "They are either African-American, Mexican-American, Italian-American, Cuban-American. So how can you live the American dream if you are trying to be something else? Everyone is trying to find themselves."

One response comes from a Dallas man, accurately summing up the tension many people tell us now faces the nation. Many Americans, he claims, seem to be "looking for differences and dwell on differences. They don't realize that they can say 'I am going to take you for the person that you are and work with you the way I can work with you.'" Yet at the same time, most people say there is great importance in "preserving our unique individuality." When such comments are made, others around the table do not disagree, even amid their concern that far too many of us continually seek to create differences and divisions among ourselves. A common point — for example by a Des Moines man — is that "everyone has got their own uniqueness. Everything has got something totally different to offer. Each and every one of us has something totally different to offer." It is cause for celebration.

Yet, despite the need to recognize people's unique qualities, participants are clear that if Americans can retain their sense of individuality only by highlighting the differences among themselves, it will create a divisiveness that challenges the country at every turn. "I, I, I!" says one exasperated Philadelphian, "When are we going to start saying We! We! We?"

THE MISSING CORE

But "getting to we" will be difficult given the profound sensation Americans now experience of being bombarded and overwhelmed and indeed manipulated by the messages, behaviors, and values that they see shaping current American life. This inundation goes beyond the annoyance that we found in 1995. People assert that these messages overwhelm them and their children, producing a nation different from the one they cherish and seek.

People say they are uncertain now as to even the kinds of relationships they might have — should have — with others outside their immediate clans or pods. As one Dallas man puts it: "People have become disillusioned, so they resort to the me-and-mine sort of thing." (In other research I have done, I have found that Americans consistently say that the values of materialism and consumerism have crowded out values of family, community, faith, and responsibility.) Troubling to these Americans is the sense that so many people now seem to confuse money with worth, replacing personal relationships with financial ones.

People tell us repeatedly that they see many Americans, themselves included, getting squeezed out economically, while too many of us too often focus just on ourselves. In these conversations, people tell of America being reduced to the economic extremes of "the haves and have-nots." "We live in an hourglass society," says one woman in Philadelphia. "We've got a lot of people with a lot, we've got a lot of people with absolutely nothing, and we've got very few people left in the middle." What seems to emerge over the course of each of our conversations is not the sense that the so-called middle class is disappearing, but rather that the "middle" of America itself is being lost along with the essence of sensibilities and values lodged there. This theme, although usually unspoken, nonetheless reverberates from town to town. One Memphis man expresses what many people feel when he notes about America nowadays, "There are gaps — widening gaps — be they political, social, economic, religious or ethnic."

To this feeling of a country being split in two, people attach many of the concerns voiced in previous sets of conversations. People now see corporations and businesses as increasingly remote, wielding a kind of undue and unwanted influence that is utterly changing what we as a nation value. "It's all about capitalism," says one woman from Memphis talking about business and the economy. She continues by arguing that the nation's *economic* mind set has become "the ruling religion in America." And while people are quick to point out that they support American capitalism — because, as one person puts it, capitalism "drives the economic engine in this country" — still, people fear deeply that America has become a greedy nation obsessed with material goods, losing a sense of control and discipline. One woman from Des Moines, using a phrase we had heard in several earlier conversations, describes the greed she sees in this way: "I want what I want when I want it."

Many people say that they also feel betrayed by political leaders who seem to act primarily in their own self-interest. One term they use to describe political leaders is "hypocritical"; another is "very untrustworthy." People see the political system and those inside it as disconnected from the needs of ordinary people and focused only on the short term. "They listen to you to get elected, then they forget you," says a Richmond man. Others share similar views, this time, a man from Des Moines: "Look at our government — the president, speaker of the house — they don't assume responsibility for their actions, but they expect everybody else to." The outrage that he expresses about double standards is palpable throughout all the conversations.

Not surprisingly, people share some unfavorable views of the news media as well. People continue to reject the argument that the news media are simply covering what is going on in communities; instead, to them, the images flashing across their televisions and playing out on the news pages are the result of intentional news media choices — and they question the basis upon which those choices are made. They say that the news media act in ways that skew and distort people's perceptions of reality. Indeed, they draw connections between the kind of reporting they see and the growing isolation they feel in their lives and throughout their communities. "The reporting of crime instills a fear in people that really hurts communities," says one woman from Los

Angeles. "The media sees too much of what is wrong instead of the things that are going right," comments one woman from Philadelphia. Others in the group agree, with one individual saying: "The media exaggerates and people are afraid."

What passes, then, for American life today fails to reflect what people want — a society of trust and common effort and shared expectations. And participants tell us that the harsh messages, the troubling behaviors, and the self-centered values that shape and drive their lives are unavoidable. So they retreat.

THE LOST PLACE

People also tell us that technology itself is increasingly becoming a force that rocks the foundation of who we are, how we interact, and the very essence of what it means to be human.

No doubt, some are expressing economic fear — a feeling that could be heard throughout the nation and not just among the participants in these discussions — that the burgeoning use of technology within the workplace is leading companies to value people less and less. One Seattle man suggests that in this technological age we look at people simply as machines, echoing a concern about the dehumanizing of society that grips many people in our conversations. He says he would "like companies that treat their employees as humans, not as machines." A similar sentiment is expressed by a woman from Los Angeles who fears that "we're going to go into a society where we are robots." And in Seattle, one woman observes: "It's going to be the technology and . . . the corporate world: they're going to be bringing people in at the low end, they're not going to be bringing them in at the high end anymore."

Moreover, people say through the advance of technology we Americans have created a society in which we no longer need to interact with or talk to each other directly, even when sitting side-by-side. They point to the sheer explosion of Walkmans, micro-TVs, cellular phones, and other "personal electronics" that can connect people and information from thousands of miles away yet allows people to ignore the person sitting directly next to them. "We are sitting at a computer terminal E-mailing to somebody, instead of actually, physically, writing a letter or going to meet them," notes one Los Angeles woman.

Indeed, as one man from Memphis observes, people often forget that "we are part of nature." He continues, "We see ourselves as above it, and ... we tend to forget it. We lose something in terms of our humanity."

For many people, the relatively recent burst of technology, and its dramatic reshaping of the American landscape, holds out great promise for a better future, with possibilities for improving education, personal relationships, entertainment, and child rearing. But the picture is not clear for people in 1998. People in our conversations no doubt see technology as progress; they are not so-called Luddites. But throughout these conversations, as people worry over the many issues and concerns that matter to them, they wonder just what effect technology is having on us as individuals and collectively as a people. Where is our human touch, a sense of humanity? Where is the nation we seek to become?

As high-tech puts people in touch instantaneously, the very sense of place, with its local institutions and routines that have helped to form and spur trust in American life, now seem to be out of people's reach; at times, people pronounced these touchstones dead. Their absence deeply troubles people, surrounded as they are by vast and rapid change. For it is these touchstones that help people make sense of the world around them and enable them to create connections to the world.

People speak of the transient nature of American society and the effect it has on the nation's life and people's sense of place. In Denver, one man notes, "There's not nearly as much sense of community as there used to be." When the discussion turns to the definition of community, he responds by saying, "watching out for your neighbors' property and they watch out for yours." There is reciprocity involved. As one woman in Los Angeles explains, it is where "everyone in the neighborhood really watches out for everybody . . . it's a sense of unity."

People say that the more Americans move around to follow jobs, the more everyone's sense of community is weakened. They now struggle to balance the demands of jobs and changing locations with the basic needs of making a community. While people explicitly point out they are not looking for "Mayberry," as one woman in Richmond put it, they do yearn for a place of belonging and familiarity and sense of continuity.

THE LOST COMMUNITY

According to some participants, even money seems to be transient these days, moving faster through a community than it used to, affecting the nature of the place in which people live. According to one Dallas man, "The money stayed in an area much longer when it wasn't just 'the hood,' it was 'the neighborhood.'" Indeed, people once called "the neighborhood" home, but today many say they fear the "hood." People lament how their neighborhoods and communities have changed from "being a place where people watched out for everybody" to a place where "the only common experience we share is that we live there," as a man from Memphis put it.

The sheer scale of life also troubles people. More simply put, people say they have lost a sense of control over their surroundings, of the place where they live. They cannot put their arms around it, so to speak, because too often it has become so large and unwieldy. People in these conversations talk about the number of people around them — the density that permeates their daily lives. "With more and more people, the closer we're pushed together, there's more need to insulate ourselves from other people," says one man in Richmond.

People tell us over and over again that this feeling of increasing density has caused numerous problems: crime, an inability to plan, overcrowded schools, fear. Seeking to explain this situation, various folks reach back to basic psychology. One participant remarks, "Remember the psychological test of crowding rats together . . . and when you crowd 'em, they become disorganized? To some degree this is what we're doing with a huge metropolitan area." The results from the rat race — indeed, from the sheer number of rats — are taking a toll on Americans.

What is more, people identify specific decisions in modern American history as contributing to the nation's diminishing sense of connection. As a man from Richmond states, "They took prayer out of school, then took the Pledge of Allegiance away so people don't feel like they have allegiance to the country." For the people in these conversations, it is a short step from removing moral markers to get to where folks see the nation today. "If you don't have those morals and the allegiance to your country and to your fellow man, then you don't know that's why our government has these problems. Everybody is out for their own," says the same Richmond man.

And people speak of their schools, which they use to see the very reflection of what people value in their community. But these Americans consistently tell us that schools no longer reflect who they are — or think they are — nor do they reflect the kind of society they want to have. One man from Los Angeles says: "We won't find the answers until we can find a way to return the schools to the community." He continues by urging, "Let us become one community, one country again." "Education," we are told by a man in Des Moines, "is both a right and a privilege," but he remarks that many people now feel that some have greater privilege than others — demanding services for *their* children or moving their children to a private school.

There is too a lingering concern that America is not educating the whole child — again the echo of an ever-present concern about the human side of life, of humanity. "You need to learn to not only do the job you want to do, but how to communicate with those people around you," says a woman in Seattle. Many people claim that the failure to provide such an education adds up to "an educational crisis." They note that some parents are unwilling or are unable to work to improve a situation that seems irreparably broken.

Navigating all these changes in American life is harder, people say, than in years past because there is no longer the same continuity of life — of guidance and wisdom — that comes from having generations of people living nearby. Layers of family life now live hundreds, if not thousands of miles away. People say that they have lost a sense of belonging and place that was created when more generations lived in the same area, or even in the same home. "You don't have the continuity, you don't have elders helping to watch your kids." A man in Dallas notes that he often thinks "back to when mothers provided moral support and the fathers provided consequential actions. We're without the consequences now."

Americans typically regard the nation's youth as a metaphor for the future, and today, when the participants in these conversations look at young people, they see a bad omen. Many said that Americans are raising children in dysfunctional families and instilling the children with unrealistic expectations — leaving them unable to distinguish reality from fantasy. "Kids get confused, and they tend to see what other kids are doing and what they see on TV, and they think that's the way," said one man in Texas. Taken away by long hours at their jobs or by separation and divorce, "parents are not putting in the time," adds a Dallas woman.

People explain that parents now try to make up for lost time with their kids by loading them up with material goods. This leads one woman from Des Moines to say, "Adults and children — our society — don't believe in themselves, they don't care about anybody else. They live for today because tomorrow might not ever come." Indeed, many people in these conversations speak about the nation living in a kind of fantasy so as to fend off reality.

People's frustration with American life is growing in response to the changes they see. They sense that the nation as a whole simply is tinkering around the margins of the challenges at hand. Many people said that time is of the essence. "If we don't get this stuff turned around, my feeling is within another five or ten years, we are all going to have to be armed, because we are just out of control," claims one Angeleno.

So, people retreat.

FORTRESS MENTALITY

People in these conversations volunteer that they are troubled by the current atmosphere of insulation, because, as a Dallas woman says, "that's just more isolating people from other people." A woman in Memphis remarks, "It's just another line of demarcation . . . separating people." And a Seattle man puts it this way: "It's unfortunate. It's a sign of the times."

People fear that the fortress mentality now permeating society is forcing people to build walls so high that they now resemble prison walls. But there's a modern-day twist to the story. "In recent times," a man in Memphis says, "you built walls to put the bad people in. They're not controlling our problems that way, so we're building walls to keep the bad people out." He also believes that there is a futility in all this, because "you don't know that the good people are in." One Richmond man tells us that the search for safety behind walls reminds him of another time in history: "It's almost like going back to medieval times when we had the castle, and everybody, when they needed protection or needed food, went to that castle." But, another man laments, it has come to the point where "there's no sense of community anymore. Everybody is walled off from the neighborhood."

When questioning people about what they think of Americans moving increasingly to planned communities, gated communities, and smaller towns, people quickly tell us why and, in doing so, often report that they themselves had made such a move, knew someone else who had, or could see the wisdom in it. "A lot of people moved out because they said they wanted to get away from the crime," states a Denver woman. Many people suggest that they and others seek cover because they believe they can find not only less crime but also "less traffic," "lower violence," "a safer place to raise kids". . . "just a little peace" . . . "a slower pace of life" . . . "a greater sense of control."

But many participants believe that when people isolate themselves and their families they are not protecting themselves from what they hope to avoid. "The problem is that crime and other things are catching up with them," observes one Denver woman when speaking of people seeking to "get away." She continues, "We're not solving anything!" A Richmond man says that all we are creating is "little birds in gilded cages." He suggests that people's attempts to escape would simply mean that "you would be locked up in your own community, putting blinds over your eyes and trying to ignore it all."

These Americans express great fear and regret that in attempting to gain control, people are actually planting the very seeds for future problems. A woman in Dallas, like so many people in our conversations, puts the problem in terms of children. "They're not going to be able to fit into society. They're not going to be a whole child. How are they going to fit into society?" And another Texan observes, "If you can't deal outside the gate, then you can't really live."

Instead of simply beating a hasty retreat, people argue, the nation — indeed, they themselves — must begin to deal with the very issues that cause them to withdraw. "We should remove the reason that is forcing me to move into this gated entity," states one Richmond man. People are clear that there is no single reason at work for the current dilemma — there are many reasons, and indeed people often feel simply overwhelmed or intimidated and end up retreating even further. It is, in essence, a "catch-22," according to one participant.

People expect Americans to do whatever it takes to regain their sense of control — sometimes to retreat, even against their better nature.

FREEDOM AND REGULATIONS GONE AWRY

We were not initally looking for a discussion of values, but their influence is inescapable and becomes more distinct with each passing conversation. It is in the discussion of values, thoughtful and often nuanced, that we see people struggling with their own uncertainties and ambivalences.

The values at play have no doubt existed in America since the nation's inception — perhaps, in fact, for people throughout time. They concern how we choose to live, make decisions, account for ourselves. But what troubles participants in these conversations is that the very balance of these values is dangerously out of whack.

People speak specifically about values that have long served to motivate and shape America — the values of competition, of control, and of material success — but that now have become "super-charged." As if given vast quantities of steroids, they have grown to be grossly out of proportion, overpowering, even ugly. Values that prompted us to live by the notion "Do unto others as you would have them do unto you" — values such as responsibility, accountability, and respect — have now been sharply diminished. Taking the shortcut is often heralded as being smart and cunning. Other values — discipline, morality, and faith — have taken a back seat in the non-stop, 24-hour-a-day, get-ahead world that people describe. Instant gratification has replaced the need to work for something of value, to make a sacrifice when necessary, or to save and nurture or to have compassion for others with less.

In this struggle over the essence and meaning of our values sits a central dilemma about how to balance the individual desire to be and feel free with the need for placing limits on what seems to people to be "outrageous," dangerous, or immoral behavior. We hear over and over again from participants the sentiments of this Memphis man: "With freedom comes choice. And when people make choices, sometimes they make good ones and sometimes they make bad ones."

Americans pride themselves on their freedom to make choices. "Free to choose," "free to do whatever we want" are phrases that roll off people's tongues as they talk about what is good about this country. Yet at the same time, these people are apparently starting to wonder if Americans have bitten off too much of a good thing. People lament that the more outrageous behavior has become in our society — from schoolyard shootings to the exploits of guests on Jerry Springer's TV show, to instances of road rage — the more they wrestle with how to set limits and who has the right to set those limits. As this topic is discussed over time in one group, people become increasingly and visibly annoyed with the current situation and their inability to find a response. One man in Richmond offers the following idea with a great deal of hesitation. He says, "I'm sure it would be a dumb solution, but … um … to revert to — if you could find a good one — a dictatorship." No one laughed.

A Memphis man, seeking to prod his group, frames the dilemma in this way: "I think what we are dealing with is deciding how free we really want to be. We are starting to wonder, do we really want all this stuff on television? Do we really want this stuff available over the Internet? Do we really want this stuff to be shown in movies?"

But while people repeatedly point out that the freedom to choose has given the nation pornography on the Internet, violence on television, and a wildly litigious society, they also complain about the impossible number of laws and regulations that dictate what one can and cannot do. In Des Moines, one man sums up the situation by saying, "The whole country is over-legislated." A Denver man sees things in a similar light: "Everywhere, everything you do has guidelines."

People say that one result of this thrust toward laws and rules is that it prevents people from taking responsibility for themselves; from having to do what is right, and from the need to exercise judgment. For instance, people repeatedly talk about how laws often push parents away from one of their main duties — disciplining their children and teaching them what is "right and wrong." We hear over and over again a fear among parents that if they discipline their children, someone will accuse them of child abuse, and social services will take the children away. One woman in Seattle comments that "the government has taken away many of the rights of parents to discipline their children." In Los Angeles, folks tell us that "the government has passed laws where the parents have no authority whatsoever. You have no authority over your children." In Des Moines, Richmond, and Philadelphia, we hear it, too.

CONSTRUCTIVE CONVERSATION

People do not say that they seek to abandon all rules. Rather, it is that some rules are too complicated, irrelevant, or both; that our reach for laws, our reliance upon them, has gone too far; that we have come to regulate our lives in ways that crowd out our own need to think, judge, and act. People express dismay that the nation, in their eyes, has lost the very standards that should guide our social interactions, which cannot be controlled by rules and laws and regulations. Discussion participants say that at times people feel that their only choice is to ignore such rules; their only choice for now, they say, is to retreat.

In this context, many participants focus on the inability of people even to discuss what can or should be done about particular situations, to talk things out, and find ways to move ahead. One Philadelphia man puts it this way: "The art of conversation no longer exists." So, while we all continue to talk — at times in seemingly endless ways through television, talk radio, and shouting matches at public meetings and elsewhere — to what extent does our talk contain meaning?

Some blame "political correctness" for this problem; others suggest that no one wants to "rock the boat." Whatever the reason, the citizens in these discussions say that Americans seem to be losing both the willingness and the ability to communicate with each other. The result, people say, is that they and the nation are ill-equipped to discuss sensitive issues, "taboo topics that get you aggravated, like politics or religion," asserts one man from Denver. Folks believe strongly that we "need to start making it acceptable to talk about things," as a participant in Dallas says.

Referring to the very conversations we are having, participants tell us they are "thoroughly amazed" and "relieved" when opportunities arose to have constructive conversations. "Most of us don't get a chance to come to a place where there are ground rules, where I can say what I want, and he is not going to leap across the table and get me," says one woman in Des Moines after our conversation. Another person in Dallas agrees: "I had a feeling it was going to be a confrontational evening. I am just amazed how much we all have gone in the same direction."

In each of the eight cities we visit, people voice one message about how America must deal with the nation's challenges. To us, it is a familiar refrain, though it now had acquired something of a spiritual element that had not been as prominent before.

We must start with the individual, our participants say, for it is the individual, when all is said and done, who has lost his or her way. In America, each individual must decide what kind of nation he or she seeks, and what each must do to contribute to its making. The problem and the solution, people say, is that fundamental. In Seattle, repeating a formula we had heard in our earlier conversations, one woman maps out the process of change this way: "If you want to change the world, start with your country; and if you want to change your country, start with your state; if you want to change your state, start with your town; if you want to change your town, start with your family; and if you want to change your family, start with yourself."

THE VALUE OF THE HUMAN SIDE

The key to starting with the individual, the notion of trust, sounds the earlier theme about the touchstones closest to us. "We have a lot more faith in our individual selves and our individual relationships than we do in some of these larger systems." By starting small, many people say, they could imagine how the country as a whole could move ahead. One Seattle man puts it this way: "I see the grassroots movement communicating to the average person that they actually have power; that it's not hopeless; that they have power and they can make a difference; that there are a lot of other people out there who feel the way they do. If they can focus that energy, they can take power back to where it belongs."

People assert that the kind of change they are talking about depends on the individual actively making the decision to change. "You can't change entire groups of people, you have to change individuals, or individuals have to want to change," says a woman in Los Angeles. Working together does not carry a notion of idealistic communal love, people tell us: "You don't have to love your neighbor to treat people like people."

People say that none of this will come easily. For many people, life is simply rushing at them too fast to see the future with enough clarity to move toward it. A woman from Dallas notes: "It's an American thing — the fast-paced life. Get it done. Everything is fast. Fast convenience stores. Fast food places." According to her, even our "young people grow up fast." The rapid pace at which Americans tend to live, people tell us, affects what kind of neighbors they are, what kind of parents they are; in short, what kind of life we Americans lead.

People believe that we must go back to basics — for instance, treating each other with respect and being responsible in the roles people play (as child, spouse, parent, co-worker, citizen, friend, neighbor, etc.).

At the heart of this discussion stands an essential dimension of being: the value of the human side of life, of humanity. "The real problem is a loss of humanity and a loss of connecting with other human beings," says a woman in Los Angeles. In Seattle, some assert that the nation is already suffering from such a loss, a theme that runs throughout these conversations, "We're creating a society of little worker drones who do nothing but come out of school and fit into this cubicle of technical expertise." People say that the loss of humanity comes from a deep tension within Americans about pursuing notions of wealth instead of well-being

The struggle to balance the concrete and the spiritual surely is not new, but today, these chagrined Americans ask if the nation has cast aside its spiritual dimension. One woman in Memphis says that "America is schizophrenic," but that given our national heritage, that is to be expected. "You had one group come over for religious purposes, another coming over for economic purposes. Those two sides don't know how to get together and don't know how to work with each other.

One side wants to have a moral side; the other side talks about money."
Meanwhile, a Los Angeles man flatly states how he sees the "schizophrenic America" working itself out: "We have become more concrete
than spiritual."

People say that America did not get to where it is overnight, that
seeing positive changes will take time, and that we must start with the
individual and the need for their human touch. A Seattle woman puts
it this way, "If anybody wants anything to change, you have to put that
first foot forward." Indeed, this notion echoes in all of our conversations, as another participant notes, "Change starts with one person.
Your influence is the most powerful thing in the world. Nobody can
touch a life without being influenced, good or bad, so it's up to the
individual to make it a good influence." And a Los Angeles woman
explains, "People essentially are the ones that are going to change the
way this country is run."

A Dallas man helps to capture the essence of what so many people
are saying in these conversations across our land. "I'm not a Pollyanna,
so I'm not going to sit here and wait for all great things to come. Each
day you just have to get up and make decisions."

Amid people's retreat, among all of the worries people put forth,
there is still some sense of hope in America. Perhaps this is surprising
given the long litany of concerns and even complaints voiced by people
– and there are many. Indeed, people share the opinion that things are
neither as good as they could be nor always changing for the better;
but there is also a glimmer of a pride and a hope in these conversations
that things can be turned around. This belief appears to be rooted in
the potential that people see in the power of individuals, the ability of
time to heal wounds, and proven lessons from history.

There is a certain pragmatism about what it means to move
the nation forward — a kind of hope tempered by patience. These
Americans tell us that, "no one thing is going to fix what is wrong with

our society, because no one thing got it the way it was." Another person observes, "It is going to take time, it is going to take endless steps in order for us to get there, but it is us that is responsible."

People speak of learning from the past. Indeed, they are in search of that which is *missing*, that which they want to locate. People consistently tell us that they miss the sense of shared purpose and national unity. Society is changing around them, they do not like the results, and they are seeking to figure out just what to do about it all. They can appear, consequently, to be nostalgic.

Based on these citizen conversations, hope still seems to exist across the nation, but so too does the reality that people must step forward and engage in public matters. According to a woman in Philadelphia, "I think that we are all complacent with our little nook in life, and to a certain degree, we are all either struggling or satisfied, or trying to do our little bit, but we are not trying to resolve or solve the whole problem." She continues, "People as a whole gotta take responsibility, too. We all shift the blame on each other and everyone. Everybody has to assume some responsibility...so let's try to work on it."

In his poem, "The People, Yes," Carl Sandburg echoed the affirmation of this Philadelphia woman and of others in these pages.

> *The people say and unsay,*
> *put up and tear down*
> *and put back together again —*
> *this is the people.*

It is the people, they themselves, to whom Americans now look for wisdom and action — to put things back together again; to make the nation again; to return America to the ideal of a nation always becoming.

SEVEN

False Start

THE YEAR IS 2003

More than a dozen months have passed since terrorists hijacked four airliners, turning three of them into guided missiles as the nation and world watched helplessly. Americans are still reeling from one of the darkest days of its history.

Prior to September 11th, politics as usual had maintained its tight grip on the nation's public affairs. The 2000 election season, which initially showed some signs of improvement from previous campaigns, reflected in part in the insurgent presidential candidacies of U.S. Senators Bradley and McCain, ended up following a familiar path of overheated rhetoric and negative campaigning. Ultimately, the presidential race was thrown into uncertainty when hanging chads were discovered in Florida voting precincts. The stakes were so high and emotions so intense that both the Republican and Democratic candidates sent former secretaries of state to Florida as their envoys. The election recount that ensued gave rise to sharp criticisms of the two candidates, their staffs, the United States Supreme Court, and the news media.

Then, in the immediate aftermath of September 11th, Americans witnessed an outpouring of good will. The day after the horrid attack, members of Congress, Republicans and Democrats alike, met on the steps of the Capitol to join hands and sing "God Bless America." So many people lined up to donate blood that blood banks were soon filled. Thousands of people made donations to relief funds; millions more engaged in silent prayer for people they would never know. Patriotic hymns were sung at ballgames, concerts, and public events of all kinds.

In the following weeks and months, Americans were told in sundry ways from coast to coast that our public affairs in this land would be different. Politicians would now conduct themselves in a more civil, bipartisan, and productive manner; news media coverage would take on a more serious tone; citizens would become more involved in politics and public life, and exhibit more care for one another.

What began as the unthinkable had unexpectedly turned into an opportunity for the nation to emerge from national tragedy even stronger, perhaps more unified, and certainly more engaged.

But this was not to be the case.

THE CONVERSATIONS

These conversations were held in Baltimore, MD; Cincinnati, OH; Dallas, TX; Denver, CO; San Jose and San Francisco, CA, and Cleveland, OH. The United States recently invaded Iraq and still had troops in Afghanistan as part of the global war on terror. In August, the largest blackout in North American history hit the northeastern United States, spawning widespread stories of frustration, as well as cooperation among those affected. Near the end of the year, California voters recalled Governor Gray Davis and elected Arnold Schwarzenegger out of a field of 135 candidates to succeed him.

These conversations were part of The New Patriotism Project, a Harwood Institute initiative supported by the Pew Charitable Trusts, concerned with the conduct of political leaders, news media, and citizens during campaigns and elections. The conversations sought to identify the changes that people saw in the country after the attacks of 9/11 and to learn whether they felt that there had been any lasting, positive effects among politicians, the news media, and citizens. We also explored what it meant to be a citizen, and asked about the meaning of patriotism.

DEEPENING RETREAT

In our conversations in 1998, some five years earlier, we heard of a nation in retreat. People had turned inward, focusing on close-knit circles of family and friends. 9/11, at least momentarily, brought people out of those circles and back into the public square. But now, only two years after the attacks and the outpouring of enormous goodwill, the sense of a new beginning has disappeared. Many people now say that their fellow Americans lacked empathy for others.

People are uneasy, anxious, and apprehensive about the communities in which they live and about the nation as a whole. They are unsure where to turn for comfort and leadership. They cite a long, diverse list of ailments that beset the nation, including health care, the economy and jobs, the environment, a rising federal deficit, and government infringement on civil liberties, not to mention the expanding role of the United States around the globe. Even people who are not economically struggling see a deepening divide between the haves and have-nots. But amid this litany of concerns, no single issue worries Americans at this time more than an overriding sense of anxiety and inwardness.

One woman in Cincinnati sums up her feelings of disquiet by explaining that, "I feel anxiety or anxious feelings sometimes — not so much about what the future holds, not even so much about the economy, just about our way of life in general and how it's going overall — too much news, overabundance, over-saturation."

In all, people view the promises made after September 11th — to improve politics, make news coverage more serious, and engage citizens — as largely unfulfilled. Many people believe that public life and politics are worse today than before tragedy struck. Rather than gaining strength from 9/11 the nation, it appears, has failed to change its path of retreat.

PATRIOTISM AND FLAG WAVING

Consider the role of patriotism during this time and the nation's response to it.

The rise of patriotism that swept across the nation in response to

9/11 could be seen at the time just by looking around — by flipping on the television set, where newscasters wore tiny American flags on their lapels, or by driving down the street, where cars and homes were adorned with the red, white, and blue. Many people felt a sense of renewed spirit and purpose among their fellow Americans. According to one Dallas man, 9/11 "created this sense that America needs to rise up, join forces, take care of its own together" — adding, "and that's where the patriotism came in." He describes how this new patriotism created the conditions for people to focus on "high topics" rather than to sit back in complacency.

Where did that focus on "high topics" go, the sense of common purpose that was so frequently hailed? That same Dallas man suggests that 9/11 provided a rush of adrenaline, only to leave people feeling high and dry. "I think it created a false sense of patriotism, because it hasn't followed through. It has declined. As people were saying, it's like a spiritual high. Like, if you go back to church again, you're on this high for a little bit. I think after 9/11 we were on a patriotism high, and now it's kind of like just fallen down." Americans had found a renewed sense of civic religion, only to lose it.

People in these conversations are frustrated by what they view as a missed opportunity. They sense that 9/11 offered an opening for the nation to truly change for the better; here, after all, was a major catalytic event that had captured the attention of an entire nation. People were seemingly ready and willing to step up. And even though our participants tell us that they had been skeptical about all the declarations of renewal being made after 9/11, they had held out hope that change would come. Not too long after 9/11, their hope was dashed.

The initial wave of patriotism fizzled in what one Cincinnati woman calls "wasted words." In Denver, a man notes that "the patriotism wore thin." More distressing, many of the participants say, conditions in the country have deteriorated, and are now even worse than their pre-9/11 days. A San Francisco man says of the aftermath, "There was a sense that things, you know, it was a wake-up call. Everybody kind of woke up. And then they went back to sleep; but further than going back to sleep, things got worse."

Some participants say that the response to the attacks actually deepened their cynicism about politics and public life, as they saw politicians beginning to jockey for position, seemingly using the attacks to gain political advantage. In Baltimore, one woman says, in a harsher assessment than most, that she believes that 9/11 was, for politicians, "a great smokescreen for them to have us focus on 9/11, while they went on to do their dirty work." Another woman, in the same Baltimore conversation, puts it this way. "It wasn't a smokescreen," but, "it was a good excuse to put stuff on the back burner, and that's what they did. They used it … Has politics changed? No, it hasn't. It's right back to where it was."

In Cincinnati, we find a consensus that the conduct of political leaders had worsened since the attacks. One man in that discussion explains, "It's just finger-pointing here and there, who's done what wrong. I mean, the Democrats want to point at Republicans, [and] Republicans say you're the reason it started in the first place. They're just going back and forth." This tit for tat leaves people shaking their heads and wondering exactly what the purpose of politics is and who is to be served.

Still, despite any frustration with politics and politicians, most comments in these discussions echo those of this San Francisco woman, "I don't think they were trying to put a smokescreen in front of our eyes. But this was a short-lived zealous moment. They were really fired up and excited about changing everything because 9/11 was a very emotional event, and everybody was just caught up in emotion. But then I think we're just back to business as usual because they just sort of lost focus of why they were going to do all these exciting things they promised they were going to do."

As for the oft-noted declarations of bipartisan cooperation after 9/11, what effects did they have on people's sense that trustworthy leadership was on the way? For the worst reasons, these declarations had nary an effect on how people ultimately viewed political leaders or politics. As one Cincinnati man laments, "There's no honesty in politics. It doesn't matter how hard you try. There is never honesty in politics."

LOOKING FOR LEADERS

Americans yearn for public leaders they can trust. The question is where they will find these leaders. In Denver, a woman suggests that "Somebody has got to come along, whether it's a leader, president, whatever it may be, that can actually instill trust . . . to get people to follow and trust them. I think that would be a beginning."

Once this notion is on the table, other group participants add that the leaders would have to "mean what they say, and say what they mean" and that they would need "to be very clear" and "show they have values." Finding such leaders "will take a long time" notes a San Francisco woman.

A Denver man maintains that the conditions within which leaders operate undermine their ability to lead. "There is so much criticism that leaders get from all sides. They are forced to pick something that they can focus on — which may not be the problem at hand — and things get diverted." This is the constraint expressed by citizens and leaders alike in our work across the nation: the political process affords leaders little room to exercise good leadership.

People strongly believe that public leaders have broken too many promises. The notion of truth and honesty sits at the core of people's desire for improved leadership. As one San Francisco woman observes, "Once these politicians get into office, the things they say, the platforms that they use, they don't follow through on them ... it's not the truth. They don't bring the truth with them." This belief is widespread and deep; it troubles people.

One Baltimore man says he is looking for leaders "who don't go back on their word." He wants leaders who "haven't made a promise and then gone back on it when they saw public opinion was against it." People want leaders who do not buckle at the first sign of opposition.

They want leaders who understand their concerns, stick by their convictions, and refuse simply to put their finger up to gauge which way the wind is blowing.

Part and parcel of such leadership is not falling prey to undue influence or the temptation to pursue personal gain at the public expense. Here is how one Cincinnati woman explains the problems she sees. "I think you've got too many big businesses giving money to politicians. That's what has ruined our country. I mean, that's the way I look at politics. There's a group of people who go into politics because we need leaders; and there's a group that goes in because they have a pet project or something that they really believe in; and then there's other people who go into it for a personal gain. But I think, once you're there, even if you have the best intentions, it's a big, complicated mess."

A woman in Denver says, "I don't trust anyone as far as the senators or presidents. It's like you can't talk to them. You don't know what they're thinking. You can't trust them."

One Denver man wonders aloud, "Who can you trust?" He says, "You get the two political parties, and … all they're doing is knocking each other. They're not working for us. They could care less about us. It's what they can do for their own good and for their own party. They could care less."

Indeed, many people believe that they will not find the leaders they seek in the halls of government. A Dallas man explains that he sees political leaders as largely running programs — "the machinery of government," as he put it. He explains that much of what he believes needs to be done in the nation takes place outside of government and that leadership for this work will naturally emerge from various sectors in society over the course of time. "The kinds of things that happen outside the system of politics, that's where America's strength comes from — because leadership is not always hierarchical. Leadership is natural. So we see people emerge who galvanize people and got great things done."

Some people refer to the kinds of leaders that this Dallas man had in mind as "heroes" — individuals who do not necessarily hold any official title but who do hold the confidence and trust of those around them. This portion of the conversation echoes themes that we had heard a decade earlier. When speaking about who could be such a hero, a Dallas woman remarks, "Everyone's a hero — and people are looking for that." People are "struggling and hoping that somebody will lead us somewhere."

Another man cautions that the word hero is overused in society, explaining that people should not bestow that title upon someone too quickly. Still, he says that he interprets people's use of the word to mean the following: "What I get is, it's because people want a leader, a strong leader, someone to bring them to a safe port, to something brighter, bigger, better – it's just a struggle."

Time and again in these conversations people tell us that they lack genuine heroes in their lives — leaders to whom they can look up and who exhibit traits of honesty and trust. These are not just idle comments. When we ask participants to name a leader whom they trust to stand up and tell them about an important challenge in the country, or in their community or state, many of the rooms fall into complete silence. In fact, in many of the discussions, the name of not a single public figure comes off people's lips; and in some conversations, it is only after being prodded that people offer up any names. Perhaps in an act of desperation, one person even proposes the actor Keanu Reeves; the individual proffers that Reeves is "as good as anyone" to rise to the task. In this inability to identify heroes, we see again the extent to which the public arena holds little meaning or relevance to people; we see just how far people have pulled away.

When participants are asked what they would say to political leaders if they were to enter the room at that very moment — they shrugged. Many sit silently in their seats, seemingly thinking what one man in San Francisco makes clear: "I have nothing to say to those people."

THE NEWS MEDIA: NO BETTER

What about the news media, which, after 9/11, said they would improve their coverage?

In a variation of the theme expressed by people in previous sets of conversations, discussion participants now say that the news media are also culprits in the nation's missed opportunity after 9/11. It did not take long, they recall, for news coverage to become as sensational and misleading as ever. Some participants cite as Exhibit A the Laci Peterson kidnapping and murder case, which grabbed headlines for months on end. To them, the Peterson case is yet more proof that news coverage had not undergone any substantive long-term change. One Baltimore man notes, "If it bleeds, it leads. You've heard that expression many times, and it's true. I mean, this Laci Peterson thing, that's all we hear about!"

A man in San Francisco speaks of the increased competition among cable news stations, which offer an in-your-face presentation, often with a decidedly divisive tone,"I don't know if it existed before 9/11, but I've noticed a real polarization of the news media between Fox News and MSNBC and how they're at each other's throats – completely left and right." He continues, "It's like watching two different countries when you turn from one to the other."

But the negative tone that permeates so much news coverage is not as great a frustration as the media's continuing attention to such sensational stories as the Laci Peterson case, which people say eats away at the time for issues they genuinely care about. Says one Denver woman: "We hear about sensational things, not the taxes, not things that are relevant to our lives."

DIVERSE CONCERNS, COMMON ANXIETIES

In a democracy, what is relevant to one person may not always be significant to the next — especially at first glance. That certainly is the case when it comes to the specific concerns of our participants. Across America, we find no single issue that stands out as most important to our participants; instead, what we see is a collection of concerns, with one issue often competing with the next.

The views of the group in Baltimore are a good example. They offer a spread of answers to the question of what people see as the most significant challenges facing them and the country. "Medicare," yells out one woman, "lots of issues going on with seniors and health care." "We're at war," says another, and then a man adds, "The economy is in trouble." Other people are quick to speak of "a lot of homeless" or "unemployment" or "crime."

Answers throughout the country are similarly all over the map. A number of people speak in various ways about economic security, mentioning the stock market decline and corporate scandals, which many people say hit close to home. One Denver man notes that "greed" is a major problem. "People want their profits now and they want big profits, and they're not willing to take a long-term view."

The issue of outsourcing — the flow of American jobs overseas — stands atop many people's lists of economic concerns. While the nation's economy has shown some signs of recovery, the improvement has come without the benefit of increasing employment, especially well-paying jobs. A San Francisco woman notes that "it used to be that people were kept on the job until they retired, and people had pride in their jobs, and self esteem was high ... Now what's happening is the companies, the corporations, would rather hire a company at the lower wage to do these jobs ... there are many financial reasons to do it, but the poor American people, a lot of them are being outsourced."

Security of another kind — homeland security, a topic that zoomed to the forefront after 9/11 — is also on the minds of a number of participants, sometimes more because of irritation than fear. One Dallas man complains that the country now had to endure "security up the ying-yang." In contrast, a woman in Dallas describes her fears after 9/11 working on the 29th floor of an office building. "I couldn't do work for a month afterwards. When a plane came by, I would freak out thinking that it was going to come through the window!"

Notwithstanding such concerns, at the time of these conversations, it seems that people's fears following the 9/11 attacks are fading; on balance, people are more concerned about the threats to their economic security than about threats to their physical safety.

Perhaps there is no clear agreement on the most important issues of concern because the deepest concern involves the troubled character of their lives and the spirit of the country. While people express a near constant drumbeat of frustration about the country's inability to act on their concerns in post-9/11 America, one San Francisco woman puts the deeper issue this way: "I think people are concerned," yet there's, "really nothing you can do. No one is listening. No one is really listening." And, for the participants, that includes their fellow Americans.

The prevailing attitude in America today, according to one man in Cincinnati, can be summed up as "I've got mine, and to heck with you." He adds, "It feels like there isn't a caring in this country that there was. Either you've got it or you don't."

TURNING A BLIND EYE TO ONE ANOTHER

The distrust that people feel toward politicians, news media, and entities such as corporations also applies to their neighbors. Many speak of the declining sense of mutual care and trust between and among Americans.

According to a woman in Dallas, "Americans don't trust people anymore. Just plain and simple, we do not trust our neighbors anymore." A woman in Cincinnati comments that, unlike her experiences from childhood, "I don't see neighbors out talking."

But simply saying that Americans lack concern for each other may offer a less-than-complete picture of current conditions. People are feeling incredibly pressed by current economic conditions and the stress of outsized personal goals. Here is how one Baltimore woman describes the situation many people face: "It is stress and money issues. You know, it's hard to bring up a family. It's hard to get a good-paying job, especially for a woman. It's just that kind of stress. Finding places to live that you can afford, taxes, insurance — all of those things add up. You're thinking about all the things you've got to do, and it's not that you're angry, it's just that you're stressed."

In Dallas, a woman explains that "you think you want to help, and sometimes you don't know how to help. But I've got two kids of my own. I work full-time, and I have two kids that are involved in sports. I don't have that much time in my day — not even talking about money, just finding the time to do something if I knew what needed to be done is too much."

Indeed, many people say that they do not have the time or energy or inclination to care about others. This is a theme from one conversation to the next. A Baltimore man simply says, "I don't have time to be empathetic."

Comments about stress, busyness, and the daily demands of life flow naturally into dissatisfaction with the lack of involvement in public life. Many people believe that after an initial surge of heartfelt activity in the wake of 9/11, individual Americans, much like the leaders and news media and others in society whom they roundly criticize, returned to business as usual. As a Baltimore woman notes, "9/11 hit, and everybody really cared. But then little by little, everybody's back into their own life, their own thing. Everybody's back into their own little life."

In making their way back to their circles of families and friends, people search for answers when asked what would have prompted them to stay engaged in public life. A Dallas woman takes personal responsibility for "not maintaining" the spirit that once flourished after 9/11. She admits to telling herself at the time, "'I'm going to go do this, and I'm going to go to that. I'm going to go volunteer. I'm going to do something!'" But she tells us, "I didn't do it. I thought about it, and then time passed. It's back to the same old, same old."

More often than not in these conversations people say that their fellow Americans choose to turn a blind eye to those around them, saying that to alleviate the trouble of others is too difficult when people feel the weight of their own troubles.

Listen to this Dallas man who says, "Me, I'm too busy in my personal

life, and I feel this is the same way with a lot of Americans. That's why
they don't get involved. They're too busy looking after themselves to be
worried about what's going on over there. I've got to make sure I make
money so that I can pay my rent tomorrow."

There is also a concern that people are stretched because of their
desire for material things. In Denver, a woman notes that "everything's
faster, and it's harder to get the money to have those things." A man
responds, "Everybody lives beyond their means trying to keep up with
the Joneses." In fact, in many of the conversations people say that they
are trying to maintain a certain lifestyle based on high expectations —
they want a big house, a sport utility vehicle, nice vacations. Another
woman in the Denver conversation adds, "No one wants to sacrifice …
we must work because we want this big car. We need the motor home;
we need the vacation; we need to catch up, and my friend's going here,
my aunt's going there, you know, trying to keep up with that … it
becomes a cycle, a vicious cycle."

Another possible reason for people's self-described lack of empathy
and involvement is the growing gulf they continue to perceive in the
nation between the haves and have-nots. For some people, action on this
front is required — and as soon as possible. As one man in Baltimore
says, "For some people it's going well. For some people it isn't going so
well." He adds, "There are people who have some sort of sympathy and
empathy for other people who are going through difficult times." But
there are many others who only see their own situation.

The growing divide in the nation brings to the fore the tension
people feel between protecting their own security and helping others.
As much as they do not like the divide, they want to make sure that
they are on the right side of it. And once there, people tend to turn their
backs on those who are on the other side. But this attitude troubles
some participants. For instance one Baltimore man declares, "You can't
just say, 'Well, I'm doing well!' You have to look around you and see
that some of your neighbors aren't doing so well." In Cleveland, a man
describes this disconnect as "almost like urban against suburban, like

the inner cities are faltering, and they're getting further and further back, and the infrastructure is crumbling, where everyone is moving further and further out with the urban sprawl and getting away from our city centers."

In San Francisco, one man uses the ebb and flow of substance abuse as an analogy to make his own point about the need for people to wake up and help others. He argues that eventually the nation will be forced to face up to its current maladies. He says, "They say when an alcoholic hits rock bottom, that's when they'll make a turnaround." He continues, "I just think that everyone, they're apathetic. As long as they've got a house and they've got their car and they've got their paycheck, they don't care. Maybe if it gets worse, they'll do something about it." A woman in that same discussion adds that people who feel comfortable have "a false sense of security. People don't understand how it works. You don't wait until it's too late." In response, a man says, "I think that they're just waiting."

WHAT HAPPENED TO
WE, THE PEOPLE?

The word *citizen*: what does it mean to Americans today? When asked, the vast majority of participants respond by focusing their comments on obeying laws and paying taxes. In Baltimore, one partic-ipant describes a citizen as, simply, "Someone who legally lives here." This is a similar definition to that provided by the Associated Press journalism stylebook — the word citizen is used when describing the legal status of someone in America. Another person in that Baltimore discussion group explains that a citizen is "Somebody who belongs. That's it; he doesn't have to be responsible or anything else."

A Cleveland woman says of citizens that "you have your rights of free speech and freedom and safety … but most people don't even think about responsibility, let alone do anything about taking on responsibility."

In most conversations it is only when prodded with follow-up questions — such as, "Is there anything more you would like to add?"

or "Can you think of anything else?" — that discussion participants ever suggest that the meaning of "citizen" requires the need to become informed on important public issues, vote, join civic groups, or care about others.

A San Francisco woman has a terse response to the question of what it means to be a citizen, saying, "I can answer it with one word: apathy. I am seeing so much apathy from people, it's almost like they're brain dead. They don't stick up for their rights." Then, making reference to the display of patriotism after 9/11, she continues: "A lot of the people that you pass by their houses, you see flags in the windows, they don't vote. People are not exercising their rights and their powers."

Some people say that while 9/11 prompted people to re-engage in politics and public life at least temporarily, there exists confusion among people about what it means to be truly involved. One Dallas man makes this observation: "I think a lot of Americans think they're a whole lot more involved." He adds, "They go out and buy a sticker of an American flag and put it on the back of their car, and they think they're doing a lot." A Cleveland man makes much the same point about writing a check to a favorite charity. "People will send a check, but they can't send their souls, they won't send themselves."

The message is clear: many people will engage but only so far. And while people may have an innate sense of civic responsibility, they are reluctant to step outside of their homes to make good on their obligations to each other.

Concerns about citizenship do not stem solely from the perspective that some people equate buying American flags with deep and meaningful involvement. There is concern as well that Americans confuse being a citizen with being a consumer. Perhaps this outlook should be no surprise. After all, in the days after the 9/11 attacks, one of the suggestions made to the American people for how they could speed up the nation's recovery was to go shopping — to purchase big-ticket items such as cars and appliances.

One Denver woman, talking about what it means to be a citizen, observes: "I think we've become customers. We're not active participants. We just show up and … get our allotment of whatever we're getting."

To pick up on a phrase used in several previous conversations, it seems that people increasingly expect to get what they want when they want it. Advertisements proclaim that we live in an "on demand" world. This commercial realm has now not only encroached on the public realm, it seems to be a major force in defining it. People routinely make demands on their local government, school system, and other institutions absent any apparent sense of personal or collective responsibility. A man in Denver observes, "It seems like we want instant gratification, we want other people to gratify us, and we want it right now." This "on demand" world breeds customers, not citizens.

One Baltimore woman sums up the distinction between customers and citizens by saying, "Customers consume, citizens create." Another woman in Cincinnati explains the difference by saying that "customers are passive, citizens are active." People repeatedly say that too many Americans are not active enough and satisfy their citizenship only by choosing to fly the flag or sending a check to their favorite cause.

It is this tension that pulls at people today. One Dallas man captures the tension in this way: "On the one hand, we all aspire to build a better community," recalling the post-9/11 expectations, "You know, the members of Congress are all going to start working together, and we're all going to help our neighbor." But on the other hand, "We're concerned about ourselves. We are concerned about our own SUV. We're concerned about our own situations. We don't seem to have the capacity to manage both. So we have this split state of mind."

In the aftermath of 9/11, one Denver woman found a glimmer of hope. She offers the following suggestion of how to create a tipping point whereby people would care more about others and be more involved. "I think we need to touch people more, and I think the reason that worked so well after 9/11 was that people actually got out into the community and helped move the rubble or like opened up the soup kitchen and fed the person." She then adds, "I'm as much to blame as anyone else. But we need to get off of our butts, turn off the television, and get out into the community, and that's not so easy."

In Dallas, one woman expresses concern that too many people are looking out only for themselves, and places responsibility for civic action on people sitting in the room that evening. "Why can't we just all go out right now and do something? We sit here like we really want to. I think what it would take would be just a bunch of people like us." Then, pointing around the table to others, she outlines the strategy. "I get ten people, you get ten people.... It's time and it's money, and it's involvement. It's taking action."

Still, many people struggle with this dilemma: "If I step forward, will others join me?" They wonder whether we, the people, are committed to addressing our common concerns. They are suspicious of promises made. The frustration level is high; the temptation to retreat is strong. False hope only deepens their retreat.

The truth is that people still hold deep aspirations for themselves and the nation. Fulfilling these aspirations, however, will not be easy. People are looking for leaders of any kind, from all realms in society, whom they can trust — who will tell them the truth, give them the straight story on bad news, offer ideas on what needs to be done, and bring others together. But where are these leaders to be found?

Meanwhile, more and more people choose to live their lives within circles of their closest friends and relatives. They shut others out. Once people came to see that the nation was not going to fundamentally change after 9/11, they retreated even further than they had at the end of the 1990s.

This is how Americans view themselves and their country. In the immediate aftermath of 9/11, they had seen an opportunity for change; in the months and years that followed, they saw that opportunity squandered.

OUR WAY BACK

EIGHT

Squaring with Reality

N ow that we have heard the people's voices, let me acknowledge what is plainly obvious: the news does not seem good
— at least at first hearing.

These conversations indicate that people have retreated into close-
knit circles of family and friends. The conversations tell us of a time
of broken covenants, unspoken truths, and failed politics. It is a time
when society is further fragmenting, and people are feeling increasingly isolated from a larger social fabric. People are in search of some
semblance of control over their lives, and with few relevant choices
before them, they have chosen a path of retreat.

FINDING THE PATH FORWARD

The question is can we do anything to reverse the people's retreat?
I believe we can. But to do so, we must pause in our mad dash of daily
activities long enough to listen carefully to people's voices and to open
ourselves up to matters that we may not wish to hear or heed.

This point is worth underscoring. For, despite the bad news of
this book, and there is much bad news, my message is not one of an
increasingly gloomy future, as I suspect some might conclude. At the
same time, I would insist that we cannot afford to don rose-colored
glasses through which we see an America where all is well. We are
indeed in trouble, but it is not, I believe, beyond our ability to change.

I believe that to find the path back from the people's retreat we
must be guided from the outset by two key perspectives. First, we

must actively embrace people's realities as the starting point from which to rethink their engagement and trust in the public realm. To do otherwise would be to risk undertaking endeavors that miss the essence of people's concerns, and that potentially might push people farther away from the public realm. By ignoring the essence of the reality they perceive — a reality that far too many Americans tell us has been routinely mangled and distorted in public affairs — we risk deepening people's sense of frustration and lack of hope.

Second, I believe that we must turn our urgent attention to the messages of hope that can be found in these conversations and let them guide our next steps. For amid the sounds of retreat, one can hear the makings of what it will take for people to step forward. If we take the time to listen, we can learn something essential about this opportunity. Our task is to locate the right openings through which we can pursue an alternate path for politics and public life.

HOW MUCH OF A RENEWAL?

At the outset, we should also acknowledge that some people and organizations have already begun to pursue this alternate path.

They have been striving throughout the nation to design new opportunities for people to involve themselves in politics and public life. I count my work and the work of my organization among these efforts. And since you are reading this book, I would bet that you too have seen or been involved in such initiatives.

Now, there are some observers who would make the claim that these efforts are on the way to producing a kind of civic renewal in the nation, the same kind of renewal we sought to explore in the 1998 conversations. The proponents of civic renewal point to some striking evidence: the rise in volunteerism in the nation since 2001; the high voter turnout in the 2004 presidential election; the millions of people who have recently engaged on issues of common interest with various groups via the Internet; the rise of the new news media, such as Web logs and innovative citizen-journalist media efforts; the scores of local civic engagement initiatives that have bubbled up across the nation; and the impressive successes of relatively new national organizations that are committed to building armies of young people volunteering and building communities.

In the face of such evidence, I have heard advocates of a new civic renewal say that I am too "pessimistic" about the nation's state of affairs; that I should take a closer look at what is happening around me. They suggest that my vision is off.

But my vision is fine.

While their argument is intensely attractive — who wouldn't want to believe that we are a nation in a time of renewal? — I still conclude that any claim of "renewal" is premature. For the clear fact is that these efforts, however promising, are taking place largely within pockets across the nation, pockets that are too small, too few, and too fragmented to shift the negative forces that now shape how Americans view and experience politics and public life. I further claim that any attempt to convince ourselves that more action has taken root than is actually the case will lead us to take our eyes off the very reality we must now confront — one of much discontent and retreat.

There are also those who suggest that 9/11 was a major positive turning point in the nation's engagement in public affairs. To them, I can only say that I wish it were so. I believe the conversations we have just listened to show indisputably that promises that resulted from that September day have had little lasting resonance with people. Our discussants made clear that, in their view, while a broad new opportunity emerged from the tumult of 9/11 — to change politics, news media coverage, and people's engagement — and while it was an opportunity they wish had been seized, it was a false start. As they see it, the promises made in the wake of that tragic day have gone largely unfulfilled.

I would add that in various in-depth discussions I have held with Americans since those reported in this book, the feelings among citizens about the missed opportunities from 9/11 have only calcified. A Cincinnati man in one group discussion said to me in May 2005, "I don't know. I just think that 9/11 made people realize maybe more that there was a common good, and then we forgot it. A couple of months later, we forgot."

OUR INGRAINED NARRATIVE

Here is the reality that I believe we must face.

When one listens carefully to the people's voices, one discovers in play a powerful narrative about politics and public life, a narrative that has taken form bit by bit, with each passing year, one layer placed upon another. In the years covered in this book, there is no sharp departure from one set of conversations to the next, nor is there a fundamental shift in tone at any particular moment in time. Rather, there has been a continuing story, with changes in emphases here and there. It has been a single narrative, built around a cluster of concerns, emotions, and issues.

Each time I go back over these conversations, I hear again the unfolding nature of people's negative views toward politics and public life, their ever-dwindling sense of community, their increasingly tenuous relationship to one another.

I hear again and again the following, sometimes even contradictory set of themes:

- People now believe that political leaders and the news media — two pillars of politics and public life — are self-serving and fundamentally not to be trusted.
- People hold that the basic values they cherish — such as forth-rightness and personal responsibility — are routinely violated in a society more concerned with instant gratification and the quick fix.
- They believe that the American dream is slipping beyond many people's reach, and the result is a growing divide between the rich and everyone else.
- At the same time, individual Americans have increasingly devoted their energies to seeing themselves as free-lancing

consumers, on their own, coveting material goods. Too many people have abdicated their personal and civic responsibilities.

- Amidst this broad discontent, people, as we repeatedly observed, have sought refuge among circles of family and friends as a way to ward off the ill effects and irrelevance of politics and public life and to regain some semblance of control over their lives.

- As we saw, September 11th seemed to open a door — people viewed it as an opportunity to reverse these troubling trends in America — yet the large promises made in its wake went substantially unfulfilled, and the result was more of the same, only more so.

What especially troubles me is how people's views seem to have cohered into an ingrained narrative about politics and public life. These views have become articles of faith among people. Over the course of this decade, these views have evolved as people's emotions have evolved — from anger to a felt-unknown, from lament to retreat, and then from the promise following 9/11 to the dissappointment of a false start. Now, rather than starting from the position of giving others the benefit of the doubt in our public affairs — whether political leaders, news media, or fellow citizens — people begin conversations on politics and public life with the expectation that things have soured and will turn out for the worst.

The pervasiveness and power of this ingrained narrative should not be underestimated. My own experience working with people in communities trying to help them clear the way to improve their collective condition is that the ingrained narrative about public affairs comes to permeate everything they do. It builds its own momentum, passing from one person to the next, as though contagious. Once it has taken hold, it is often taken for granted as accepted wisdom, usually without much critical inspection. The lines of the narrative come to be repeated like the refrain of a popular song. And when they are invoked, few people stand up to say that the narrative may not always be true, or that there are examples of people or organizations that defy current trends.

The effect of the ingrained narrative is to undermine people's sense of possibility and hope in the public realm. The narrative suggests that change is not in the offing, sometimes not even possible.

Not long ago, in another set of discussions that occurred after this book was largely written, I asked people to imagine ten years from now what would need to change in America if their aspirations for the nation had been acted upon. I can remember in one group conversation, a man sitting across the table from me who found it nearly impossible even to entertain the question. He could not imagine how change could come about. Eventually, he did answer the question, but only after I had actively engaged him a number of times, in a number of different ways.

BUSY AT HOME, AWAY FROM THE PUBLIC SQUARE

No doubt, the trends that I have identified in these pages began long before I started to engage Americans in these conversations. Exactly when, though, is hard to say.

It is nearly impossible for me to pinpoint the exact time when people began to turn more inward and retreat from the public realm. Still, in my own research and projects, I can recall picking up signs of these trends in the 1980s. At the time, there was an increased emphasis in society on notions of personal fulfillment; the language of market-based policy and politics took greater hold in our national affairs; and the rise of the young urban professionals, better known as "YUPPIES," became squarely lodged in our consciousness as examples of conspicuous consumption throughout society — all signs of movement away from the public square.

Others might say that the cluster of trends I have identified here, and perhaps other associated trends, came in response to the experiences of the 1970s, when Americans endured revelations about Watergate, long lines at gas pumps, and the ongoing Iranian hostage crisis, to mention only three significant events of the period. This was the time, according to some pundits and observers, that a sense of malaise came over the nation.

And still others will point out, and rightfully so, that the nation has undergone various swings in people's engagement throughout the country's history, and that the period which I am exploring in these pages will certainly not be the last of such swings.

But such hunting for the precise "why" for our current situation takes us away from our task today. For whatever the changes that led up to the period of my conversations, and whatever the changes that took place during the period of the conversations, people's voices, shifting emphases aside, remained remarkably *consistent*. The narrative stayed firm. This was a period, remember, when public opinion surveys about whether Americans felt the nation was on the right or wrong track variously peaked and dropped dramatically in relationship to such changing events as the first Gulf War, the economy's record-paced expansion, September 11th, and the fall of Baghdad. Yet, the pattern in these conversations remained the same: a steady, growing, and deepening retreat from politics and public life.

This pattern held true even as many people have told me about their incredibly busy — albeit often overstressed — lives. There have been many articles and reports documenting Americans' frenetic schedules, filled by a host of activities — from volunteering to book clubs to kids' ballgames to engagements with their religious institutions. And yet, even as people rushed from one activity to the next, and even though some of these activities show local civic involvement, they told me that they were withdrawing from politics and public life. They felt that a change had occurred in their civic involvement and was continuing. They felt as though they were closing down, moving away from the public realm.

The focus on the personal, or at least on the familiar, was amplified throughout these conversations. Here is another example: The explosion of new gizmos and gadgets that have enabled us to connect to people who are hundreds of miles away yet allow us to ignore the person sitting directly next to us or living next door. Indeed, how many times have you seen people standing in a crowd, or in line at a store, with their ears attached to their cell phones or with their MP3 headphones on? As people in these conversations have pointed out, we are all highly connected — the question is, to whom and toward what end? New research indicates that more and more Americans are now moving to geographic areas to find like-minded people. Increasingly, Republican areas are becoming more Republican; Democratic areas more Democratic. The change is not further evidence that one of our biggest problems today is a polarization within society based on political party; I have already argued that that is not the case. Instead, the point is that we are surrounding ourselves with those with whom we feel comfortable. Even if we are creating incredibly robust lives for ourselves, we risk separating ourselves from anyone, even next door neighbors, who are not like us, and circumscribing our associations by close-knit circles, technology, and geography.

TAPPING THE POWER OF THE INDIVIDUAL

At the beginning of this chapter, I proposed that if we listen closely enough to these conversations, we will discover the basis upon which we can find a way back from our retreat.

Let me start this part of the discussion by outlining why I believe so strongly that people are willing to engage in politics and public life, especially after I have invested so much time and energy in detailing people's retreat. Consider these items:

- Americans over these 15 or so years have been fully aware of their own failings — they have consistently pointed out their own retreat from the public realm, from each other, and from their civic responsibilities. Such awareness is essential for any kind of change to occur within individuals, groups, or communities.

- By the end of these conversations, it becomes clear that people's emotions are rooted more in regret than in anger. They are saddened by the current state of affairs and express the desire to change course. Indeed, they aspire to more constructive relationships and action within politics and public life in the nation.

- People say that changes in direction of the nation must start with the individual — with people themselves taking responsibility for stepping forward and making a difference. They sense that the problem in America certainly includes public officials and the news media, but it extends as well to themselves and others in their communities and in the nation as a whole.

- Citizens suggest that people's character — its definition and its expression in daily life — must play a central role in reversing our individual and collective retreat to improve the condition of the country. Thus, the challenge is not simply about improving voting systems or finding legislative fixes for a particular social problem, though both may help, but about the exercise of individual character. This is something everyone can attend to.

- People have realistic expectations about change; they believe nothing will happen fast, that there is no silver bullet. Change will come only through a series of actions woven together over time. And many people want to start such action at the local level, where they can see people they trust leading efforts, and they can participate in and follow the progress of various endeavors.

- People are in search of everyday heroes — individuals who in everyday life demonstrate the ability to help others, make a difference, and persevere in the face of adversity. People do not believe in, nor do they want, a knight on a white horse who comes to save them.

- No matter how frustrated people are about politics and public life, there remains, still, a sense of hope within them. Indeed, in each set of conversations, no matter the depth of frustration that people expressed about politics and public life, they maintained a degree of hopefulness about our ability to pursue an alternate path for the future.

In all, these voices tell us that it is the power of the individual we must tap. Widespread change in society, the kinds of shifts people in these conversations are seeking, will occur only when we summon people's individual characters and their sense of responsibility. It will occur only when people are called forward — to step beyond their own close-knit circle of family and friends into the larger public arena.

How might this happen?

NINE

Something Larger
Than Ourselves

What I believe people are seeking, and what we so desperately need in America today, are more opportunities to engage in collective actions that seek the improvement of our condition. Too many of us have turned inward, away from one another and from the common challenges that await us. I am not suggesting in any way that people forfeit their self-interests; after all, self interest is part and parcel of human nature, and we should not pretend that altruism alone can trump it. Too often, it seems, we attempt to engage people in public affairs by pretending that we can strip them of their self-interest or by appealing to self-interest alone. This is a mistake.

I believe that if we are to tap the power of individuals in our society we must begin to engage people in ways that actively ask them to think about and weigh their interests in relationship to those around them; to see larger societal needs at work; to imagine the possibilities for what can be achieved when individuals come together to act in the public realm.

IMAGINE AND ACT FOR
THE PUBLIC GOOD

To meet this challenge, we will need *to heighten our consciousness of the public good*. This is essential. Such a course will enable us to operate in a richer framework than the mere effort to engage individuals in exercising their voices as isolated consumers choosing among assorted, discrete options intended to benefit them alone.

Wherever I go, I am asked if it is even possible for people to imagine and act for the public good. The short answer is yes — a strong yes. Indeed, when the question is put to me, I find myself filled with impatience, and sometimes angry passion. Embedded in the question is more than a passing assumption about people's retreat into family and friends and away from the public realm. What I often hear is a reflexive, deeply held (and sometimes unexamined) *belief* that Americans are unwilling, or maybe unable, to see beyond themselves; that somehow, Americans have become intrinsically selfish; that we as a people are incapable of giving of ourselves when the matter at hand does not concern our individual welfare.

I reject these assumptions.

My response comes not from some philosophical treatise I have read or from some academic course I have attended. It emerges from a much deeper and practical place: my experience in working with my fellow Americans in one community after another over the past 20 years or so.

Each time I have heard questions (and doubts) about people's ability to work for the public good, I literally see pass before my eyes the pictures of individual faces that I have met along the way, from one community to the next, their eyes lit up with concern for others, their hearts large enough to embrace the needs of many.

These are not people I would call extraordinary. They are not the superhuman volunteers we sometimes read about daily in newspapers; nor are they those individuals featured on the nightly news; their faces are not the ones plastered on the front covers of national magazines.

The people who come to mind are ordinary Americans — the kinds of everyday heroes referred to throughout these pages — who demonstrate what it means to act on behalf of the public good through their daily words and deeds. I have in mind, for instance, the people I have met in Flint, Michigan, where I have been working since 1995. These people who, despite tremendous odds stacked against them — one plant closing after another, periodic drive-by shootings, boarded up store-fronts, and abandoned lots — have chosen to stay in their community and work for the betterment of their common condition. They have come together to work on race relations and racism; improving their public schools; cleaning up abandoned lots and buildings; creating inspiring theatre productions that ignite people's imagination about their community, its future, and the role that individuals can play. Notwithstanding the enormous challenges before them, my friends and colleagues in Flint are making real progress, step by step. And they will tell you that progress comes when people discover that they are connected to something larger than themselves.

I am reminded of working on initiatives to reconnect communities and schools, one instance of which took place in Greenville, South Carolina. When we entered this community, local people told us that sharp divisions existed between African Americans and whites; people new to the community and those who had lived there for years; religious folks and so-called secular liberals; wealthier residents and those with little wealth. And yet, under the right conditions, this community, with all these cross-currents, did come together. Eventually, people figured out what they wanted for their community and their schools. In interviews conducted after the initiative was completed, people told my staff that the biggest surprise to them was not any specific action that emerged from their work together, but the mere fact that people from throughout the area could sit at the same table and work together. They told us that they realized that they shared more in common than that which divided them. They, too, could now see themselves as part of something larger than themselves.

I have seen such progress — such small miracles — in one community after another. I have in mind the people with whom I have been working in Mobile, Alabama, and in Orlando, Florida, and in scores of commu-nities across the state of Ohio, all of whom have also chosen to stand up for the improvement of public schools for all children, not just their own child. Progress is slow, but it is happening in these places.

I have seen change in major metropolitan newsrooms, civic organizations big and small, foundations, and assorted other organizations and found that, notwithstanding the difficult road that must be followed, people's individual characters can be tapped and their reflexes can change; they can engage in their public work together if an alternate path is pursued. Change is possible.

Then, I must add, there is that intriguing city of Las Vegas, Nevada, where I am also working, a community located in the middle of a desert, and one of the fastest growing regions in the entire nation. This community is opening, on average, one new school building per month.

It is clear that tens of thousands of Americans have flocked to this desert town because they see it as the last best place in America to pursue their own customized version of the American dream. Anyone can become anything! Still, after talking with the people of Las Vegas, my colleague Jill Freeman and I found ourselves writing a report about the city, *On the American Frontier*, in which we maintained that even the people of Las Vegas, as intensely independent as they are, have begun to suspect that unfettered individualism may be at odds with common needs. The people of Las Vegas, we wrote, "…yearn for all individuals to be able to pursue their own dreams and make their own way. The uniqueness of Las Vegas is rooted in this independent streak, which drives its very culture and people. But it is this insistence on independence that may now be getting in the way of what people want for themselves and the community. Amid individual pursuits, people hold common concerns — and the concerns are growing."

We summarized the situation in Las Vegas this way: "How can people be connected and work together in a fast-paced, rapidly growing community that is inherently focused on the individual?"

WHICH PATH WILL WE CHOOSE?

This is the challenge we face throughout America, not just in Las Vegas. How can each of us, as individuals, pursue our own dreams and still be connected to one another and work for the public good?

Las Vegas sits on the frontier of American life, where our tendencies as a society tend to be exaggerated, and yet even there, people express concern about how far they can pursue their own individual lives without connection to others. What is clear from the people's voices in this book is that over the past 15 years or so, Americans from communities far and wide are also recognizing the limits of individuals going it alone. It is one thing to pursue one's dream; it is yet another to find oneself circumscribed by close-knit circles that cut us off from one another.

I come away from these conversations hopeful because people are not simply laying blame and pointing fingers at others, looking elsewhere to explain or remedy this retreat. For me, the hopeful news is that as these conversations evolved over time, people came to look at themselves as playing a central role in the problem at hand and in the required solution for moving forward. People told us that individual Americans from all walks of life must assume greater responsibility for placing the nation on an alternate path.

So, we have a choice. We can move forward in one of two ways: we can see people as isolated individuals, or we can engage people as a part of something larger than themselves.

To choose the former course will fail to place us on an alternate path. It represents a variation of the current default mode of selling politics and public life as if they were one more consumer product, and will serve only to reinforce the current retreat, not to reverse it. From public schools to political campaigns, people are told they live in an on-demand world, to expect what they want, when they want it. They are approached as atomized consumers. These messages of consumerism are now so pervasive that people have come to expect them. What's more, people have built a protective barrier of skepticism around themselves, which often prevents even genuine messages from penetrating their awareness. The barriers do more than simply keep external forces out; ultimately they confine the individual to a personal space that keeps people turned inward, in the process making them indifferent, or even resistant, to their full involvement in the public realm.

We must turn our backs on this approach.

THE CALL AND RESPONSE

Today, we must make an express commitment to our connection to one another and to what matters among us. In the aftermath of 9/11, we saw glimpses of this collective commitment — to a public good — only to see it dissipate in the months thereafter.

Now, we must ask ourselves, how often do we hear references to the public good in current conversations about the challenges that confront us? How often is the notion of the public good invoked during political debate, at school board meetings, in civics classes, among neighbors? To what extent is the public good even part of our collective consciousness?

When Alexis deToqueville explored America in the 19th century, he observed that "it is difficult to force a man out of himself and get him to take an interest in the affairs of the whole state." The implication is that we cannot force or even cajole people to take a broader view in politics and public life today.

As I listened to Americans talk about the nation over the past dozen-plus years, I did not come away believing that we will succeed in manipulating people to take an interest in public affairs. Rather, I found something much more promising: people are waiting to be called back to the public square. Listen carefully to their voices and it becomes clear, at least to me, that people are in search of an alternate path back into politics and public life. They recognize their own failings; they see the need to take on greater personal responsibility; they know that they cannot go it alone; they wish for the nation to change its course.

Do not misread me.

Americans are not political junkies who wish to spend all their leisure hours discussing matters of public affairs; most do not awake early on Sunday mornings to take in the political talk shows on television; and voting levels remain a matter of concern. But listen to people's voices and you can hear them articulate a belief that they have become disconnected from one another; that their political leaders and news media have lost their public purposes; that public discourse is too divisive and empty.

There is a sense of meaning absent from our public affairs and people know that they, too, are absent.

HUMAN NATURE AND HUMANITY

Time and again in these conversations I have heard people make reference to the fact that in all the complexities of politics and public life we have seemingly lost sight of the fact that we are dealing with human beings and, as more than one person put it, with humanity itself. These are comments I have continued to hear long after most of this book was completed.

I suspect that I take a huge risk in raising the idea of humanity. I might be accused of going soft in the rough and tumble game of politics and public life, a game that is now reserved for those people with thick skins and short memories. But perhaps it is this risk that must be taken. Somehow, as the legions of consultants and pollsters, pundits and handlers, have grown, *the pre-eminence of people and their urgent needs and higher aspirations have been lost.*

This point, perhaps more than any other, sticks with me from these conversations. It is one that each of us must take forward with us as we summon ourselves and others back into public life. We have lost, or maybe just temporarily misplaced, the purpose of politics and public life. I know that some people will assert that its purpose is to win battles and arguments and positioning and votes; that without "winning" people cannot wield their influence and pursue their agenda. But, when one travels from village to town to city and listens intently to the voices and aspirations of people, that purpose rings hollow, even shrill.

I fear that in the midst of politics and public life we fail to remember that most people have an innate goodness about them; that, when given the choice, they would like to make what they believe to be are the right choices; that they would like to be viewed in good stead by their peers. Indeed, sometimes I think we forget that people want to belong to something larger than just themselves.

Some people have asked me if these notions are simply a matter of my civic faith; in part, they are. After spending my entire adult life working in communities, I do believe these notions, and I do believe they are lodged deep within each of us. Yet I have also come — even more — to know these notions through experience, by engaging in various on-the-ground initiatives, rigorous research, and travel across our land. I urge people to explore their own community and other communities and to put themselves back in touch with these basic notions about people and their aspirations. They are enormously powerful.

In the pursuit of public affairs, we seem to misplace these insights about human nature. Our tendencies play to the lowest common denominator. Our efforts work to strike fear in people's hearts; to manipulate their emotions; to generate acrimonious and divisive debates. When Americans look out over the public landscape we now have, they wonder what has happened to our sense of humanity. They know there is a different reality in the offing.

And, so, the answer lies in large measure with each individual. Will we believe in one another, in our collective ability to bring about progress, and will we tap the goodness that exists in each of us? Or, will we see politics and public life as being about manipulation, personal positioning, and material gain? At issue is whether we can, indeed whether we will, re-instill a sense of purpose and meaning in our public affairs.

TEN

What Gives People Hope

I f you listen to the people's voices, it is clear that a notion of the public good is missing from our shared lives. In this sense, the health of our public realm can not be judged simply on the basis of voter turnout, or other large-scale indicators such as the number of people who are involved in a single initiative, or who donated to a political campaign or visited a Web site. Rather, we must examine whether people see themselves reflected in the issues debated in politics and public life, how connected they feel to each another, whether they see themselves as citizens having obligations to one another, and the extent to which they believe collective action is possible — even necessary.

As I said in Chapter Two, people are stuck in a "waiting place." While they have a latent desire to engage, they are unable to locate or imagine a different path for politics and public life. Indeed, conditions in the public realm have only worsened in the period covered by these conversations. We are moving in the wrong direction. What should we do?

I have already said that we must embrace people's reality and engage individuals as part of something larger than themselves.

Now, I turn my attention to one more facet, which I believe sits at the crux of creating an alternate path for our politics and public life in this era of retreat — *affirmation of our commitment to hope.* Yes, hope! Without sufficient hope, people will not step forward and be engaged. They will not believe that change is possible. And they will not give of themselves and fulfill obligations to others. It is a renewed sense of hope that all people need in order to move out from the waiting place and to gain a sense of possibility about the future.

But what gives people genuine hope?

T H E   M I R A G E   O F   F A L S E   H O P E

Here we must make a critical distinction between authentic and false hope. False hope is what so many political leaders, news media, civic leaders, and others peddle in daily life. Sometimes this false hope is pursued in order to manipulate and win battles in the public arena; at other times, it is the unintended consequence of our actions. Such false hope is not neutral in its effects on people, somehow harmlessly washing over them. Just the opposite is true; false hope eats away at people's sense of trust and possibility within the public realm; it leads them to turn away.

The conversations I have recounted in this book remind me of another study I conducted, called, appropriately, *Hope*. In it, people talked about the kind of false hope they see in politics and public life, an image that can make public affairs seem almost cartoonish and devoid of meaning. Today, our public life is filled with elements of false hope.

False hope rears its ugly head when people needlessly inflate expectations about plans and programs and anticipated results. Sometimes they pursue this path of exaggeration because they believe it is the only way to get people's attention or to motivate them into action. While such inflated expectations may sound good at the time, when they go unfulfilled, they represent more broken promises to people. We must know that the effects of broken promises add up over time and cause people to stay put in the waiting place.

False hope is a result of "tough talk" and "pledges" that are regularly offered in politics and public life — attempts to demonstrate one's conviction or commitment, to stake out one's territory on a public concern or battle, or simply, once again, to gain people's attention. But such soundings all too often result in empty rhetoric, pandering, and double-talk. All this activity undermines a sense of forthrightness within the public realm, and engenders a sense among people that they are being played with. It leads people to feel that their reality has not been addressed, or even that it has been distorted.

The overreliance on polls, focus groups, instant surveys, and other public opinion tools also leads to false hope. The use of such mechanisms is intended to suggest to people that they have been heard. But as the conversations in this book suggest — and I believe that it is the truth — people often feel that such information is used by those in positions of power merely as fodder to manipulate ideas, positions, and speech lines, as an instrument of reconnaissance rather than as an effort to truly understand people and reflect their concerns.

False hope is created when there are attempts to "manufacture heroes" — when a person or organization's past record, performance, or sense of self-importance is exaggerated or hyped; when there is the suggestion that a single individual or group has all the answers. People know in their heart of hearts that the world is too complex for such folly and rigidity.

Importantly, false hope also is produced when people engage in self-righteous behavior in relationship to other people's weaknesses or foibles or mistakes. Such endeavors are often undertaken in the name of strengthening our collective values in society. But this approach can lead to the setting of dangerous double standards and the pursuit of a politics of personal destruction. One does not need to look very hard to see such behavior in our politics and public life; it is rampant.

Then there is the simple matter of suggesting to people that a "crisis" is upon us, used as a means to galvanize support for a new direction or action, when in fact no crisis exists. Such dire warnings seem to come and go swiftly in the public realm, often failing to gain any significant traction among people. Indeed, rather than engage people, such warnings make us numb to various pronouncements, even to those that may be real and which require our urgent attention.

Finally, there are those who seek to generate a sense of hope within people by making them feel guilty about their lack of participation in politics and public life, or their lack of support for a worthy social cause — public education, fighting hunger, providing natural disaster relief. The list is endless. The desire here is to prompt a more positive reaction in people. But when people are already in retreat, attempts to make them feel guilty only push them farther away.

We witness false hope in the public realm every day. Its purveyors, I believe, assume that they can somehow outsmart or outmaneuver people to get their attention, make them care more, move them to action. They assume that they can simply manufacture a sense of hope within people's hearts, failing to address people's real concerns. And even when they are able to get a rise out of people for a fleeting moment — during a political campaign, for example — such hope can evaporate quickly.

The pursuit of false hope only deepens the ingrained narrative of politics and public life that so many people carry with them, and which permeates our collective consciousness. It signals people to remain in the waiting place.

THE PURSUIT OF AUTHENTIC HOPE

If we are interested in the affirmation of hope, then we must put ourselves on the alternate path of authentic hope. This path requires that we bring with us the belief that people hold an innate sense of hope waiting to be tapped. It is in this belief that we will find our opportunity to change course. For the challenge we face is that people's sense of hope remains latent and unanimated. It will be ignited only by something real and meaningful. What's more, we must know that this sense of hope will grow and flower only as people see reasons to give of themselves.

At issue is whether we are willing to do what is necessary to pursue authentic hope. We have already identified key elements of false hope. The following paragraphs identify key elements of authentic hope.

To experience authentic hope, people must see signs of small steps forward, steps that build on one another, steps that create an ever-growing base of hope that will grow exponentially in time. In an era of retreat, such small steps can be more believable than promises of large-scale initiatives that too often produce few results. As I mentioned in the previous chapter, some of these small steps are taking place across the nation; now, they must grow and expand and be seen by more and more people.

People gain a sense of authentic hope when they see other people who demonstrate their convictions — who say clearly what they think and what they believe without pandering, double-talking, or pursuing a politics of personal destruction. This is a refreshing change for people, even when they do not agree with the convictions. I have often heard people express this sentiment when talking about a political candidate: "I don't like what he says, but I sure do respect him for taking a clear stand."

Authentic hope emerges for people when certain enduring traditions within the nation are exhibited — when people demonstrate the spirit of overcoming adversity and challenges, setting their sights on inspiring goals, looking for shared values, using common sense. These traditions — taken alone or together — are antithetical to the kind of manipulation and maneuvering found in the pursuit of false hope.

Authentic hope comes from seeing and engaging in collective conversations, which reignite people's belief that they can talk together and, even when they disagree, sometimes vehemently, can still make progress on common challenges. This is the story of Greenville, South Carolina, where people came together despite racial, economic, and political differences. The productive public discourse that gives people hope is a far cry from the needlessly divisive and acrimonious battles we see in our national politics and public life, and even at local school board meetings and city council sessions.

People gain authentic hope from knowing that others in the nation still care about one another and care about politics and public life. But what does this mean? We live in an era of so-called red states and blue states, when people are told that sharp differences exist, for instance, between church goers and non-church goers. These dichotomies create narratives of divisions in society; they lead to assumptions about each other that drive people's attitudes and behaviors; they produce splits within local communities and on the national scene. The effect is to undermine a sense of shared purpose among people. People gain authentic hope when they see people crossing boundaries, when they see people working toward a common goal, when they see that people will still help their neighbors.

Focusing on real concerns, rather than on trumped up issues, also gives people authentic hope. The problem today is that so many issues are framed in terms of supercharged emotions and false battle lines, where the nature of a problem is exaggerated, where choices do not reflect people's real concerns, where real costs are underestimated, and where potential results are oversold. Notions of authenticity become lost in this maze of positioning and deception.

I would make one last point concerning authentic hope: amid all the debate and heated battles over "religion" and "moral values" in America, most people I have talked with find authentic hope in a kind of secular spirituality (for some people, obviously, this includes a religious spirituality) that we can all hold in common. This secular spirituality is based on notions that people are innately good, the possibility of humankind, and a sense of belonging to something larger than themselves. When these notions are put into play, when they are reflected in the ways in which we go about politics and public life, when they are embedded in the real give-and-take of politics and public life, people gain a sense of authentic hope.

This is the alternate path we must take now.

DON'T FOOL WITH HOPE

When I talk with people about the need for more hope in politics and public life, they often respond by saying that they are already pursuing this goal. Then, when I ask how, typically they mention approaches that lead only to more false hope.

Their intentions are often sound; their own hope for change is deep. But what sits beneath their activities is a set of assumptions and practices that are, unfortunately, rooted in false hope. Indeed, many of us have been taught to embrace assumptions and practices — a kind of conventional wisdom on how to foster hope — that lead us down the wrong path. For example, none of the following approaches will necessarily produce more authentic hope on their own: undertaking more communications or raising the volume of one's efforts, increasing the frequency of what we say and do, being more empathetic, making use of new technologies and gadgets, or conducting one more public opinion survey or town hall meeting. None of these approaches will necessarily create the conditions where people will want to involve themselves in politics and public life, where they will seek to connect with others, and where they will discover their potential to make a difference and join with others to build a common future.

Too many of us are engaged in the public arena in ways that deepen and expand false hope. We must get ready to go down a different path; and we must engage others to come with us. This will require us to carefully and vigilantly examine how our own words and deeds contribute to false hope and to identify ways to engender authentic hope.

There is much to learn about the practice of authentic hope. And there are many venues in which it must be pursued — in exercising leadership, running civic-minded organizations, building communities, and practicing partisan politics. But here, in these pages, my main point is to sound the clarion call that we must become more aware of the need to undertake such an examination and to make the commitment to pursue an alternate path. For we must always remember and keep clear in our minds that hope is central to the human experience. It drives people's sense of who they are and who they can become. Hope tells us to keep going when various signs around us suggest that we should give up or give in. In an era of retreat from politics and public life, people do not want to experience more broken promises and distorted realities that undermine their sense of hope. They do not want to endure more disappointment. Professing to be about authentic hope, only to pursue false hope, will do more harm than good. It will set people back even farther. This much we must know.

IN OUR AFFIRMATION OF HOPE

Authentic hope is different from a sense of optimism — a kind of cheerful, giddy exuberance. Authentic hope emerges from a much deeper, timeless place within each of us, and within society as a whole. It finds its home in the nation's rich, inspiring history; in the demonstration of American character over time; in the ability of Americans to correct their course when proven wrong.

In our affirmation of hope, we would commit ourselves to tapping into this wellspring of American spirit. We would build on people's desire to be part of politics and public life. We would work from the assumption — born out by our own history — that politics and public life *can* change when we put ourselves to the task. We would know that we are not destined to a slow denigration of conduct and affect in the public realm that withers our spirits.

The affirmation of hope would require, too, that we cultivate within ourselves what Woodrow Wilson once called a "posture of ownership" — and, so, we would forsake the mindset that tells us we can "visit" the public square when it is to our liking or convenience, only to retreat whenever that suits us better.

In our affirmation of hope, we would no longer resign ourselves to the current maladies that afflict public affairs; instead, we would see that we have the obligation and power to act and make a difference. Indeed, in our affirmation of hope, we would come to hold ourselves to higher expectations for our words and deeds — understanding that they matter — rather than complaining endlessly about unsatisfactory conditions, or turning away in disgust, or immersing ourselves in false hope.

Much in politics and public life hinders progress and blocks our pathway. But without this affirmation of hope, where will we be?

My own experience tells me that too many of us will remain on the sidelines, spectators of public affairs, just at the time when we are needed most. Too many of us will buy into the assumption that we are powerless, when action is possible. Too many well-meaning efforts will fail to adequately address the great challenge of people's disaffection that now confronts us. And, worse yet, too many endeavors will be designed and implemented that further divide politics and public life and diminish people's hope.

The affirmation of authentic hope calls upon each of us to conduct a hard and truthful examination of our own words and deeds, and the words and deeds of the organizations or groups we lead. Then we can tap into people's latent desire to engage.

Can you hear the people's voices? Perhaps we need to remember the comment of this Orlando woman: "People really do care, even when we say we don't." And the Seattle woman who said, "If anybody wants anything to change, you have to put that first foot forward."

Then there was the Richmond man who reminds us, "If we say we're frustrated and not going to do anything about it, then we won't. But if we keep trying, we might make a difference."

The people's voices — they tell us that we must see ourselves differently if we are to find hope in an era of retreat. They tell us that we must act with authentic hope. They urge us to step forward.

ACKNOWLEDGMENTS

There are many people I would like to thank for helping me put this book together.

I wish to thank my colleagues at The Harwood Institute for Public Innovation who over the years were instrumental in carrying out many of the group conversations I report on here. In addition, I am grateful to the organizations who commissioned the research, including the Kettering Foundation, Pew Center for Civic Journalism, Knight Ridder Newspapers, and The Pew Charitable Trusts.

My colleague at The Harwood Institute, Patrick Miller, was a great aide throughout the process of writing this book. He dug back into our original research time and again, wrote up various ideas, and provided wonderful comments on the different chapters. He shepherded the entire production process.

Harris Dienstfrey was my editor. I cannot thank him enough for his ideas and thoughtfulness and grace. Through his comments and suggestions, he always improved the manuscript, while always maintaining a sense of affection for what became our common task. Along the way, Keith Melville, a professor at the Fielding Graduate University, read the manuscript. I appreciate his time and comments.

Ilse Tebbetts provided the final line edit on the manuscript. And Chris Lester, of Rock Creek Creative, designed this book. I hope you enjoy his handiwork as much as I do.

Robert Kingston, senior associate of the Kettering Foundation, provided the inspiration for this book. I had talked with him many times about this idea and always received encouragement in return.

What's more, he commented on various drafts, endlessly prodding me to better articulate the research and my arguments.

I also wish to thank John Dedrick, director of programs at the Kettering Foundation. He was the individual who ensured that this project found a home and that it came to completion. I never cease to be impressed by his level of professionalism and commitment to his work.

I am indebted to David Mathews, president of the Kettering Foundation. I am enormously appreciative of his support for this book and the many studies over the years that I report on here. I appreciate, too, his words in the Foreword. But, mostly, I am thankful for his leadership in finding ways to make America better and to make democracy work as it should.

I am especially grateful to my wife, Jackie, and my two kids, Emily and Jonathan, who have helped to make our family work as it should, especially during the period when I was writing this book while running an organization.

I must leave the last word of thanks to the scores of people I met through the conversations we held in cities and towns across America. Each time I engage people in this nation, I am reminded of the country's strength and beauty.

RICHARD C. HARWOOD

Richard C. Harwood is founder and president of The Harwood Institute for Public Innovation, a nonprofit catalytic organization dedicated to helping people imagine and act for the public good. For nearly two decades, Harwood has led the charge to redeem hope in our politics and public life, discovering how to create change in the face of negative conditions. He has developed new kinds of leaders and civic-minded organizations in dozens of communities across the country.

Harwood has devoted his energies to spreading a vision for what American society should be and putting innovative practices to use on the ground to turn that vision into reality. A frequent expert commentator in national and syndicated media, he has authored numerous studies on the vital issues of our time, including education, health care, and the state of American politics.

More about Harwood's work can be found at www.theharwoodinstitute.org

---

THE KETTERING FOUNDATION

The Kettering Foundation is is an operating and research foundation rooted in the American tradition of inventive research. The foundation does not make grants. Its founder, Charles F. Kettering, holder of more than 200 patents, was best known for his invention of the automobile self-starter. He was interested, above all, in seeking practical answers to "the problems behind the problems." Established in 1927, the foundation today continues in that tradition, but the objective of the research now is to learn how democracy can work better. Its major programs of research are designed to shed light on what is required for strengthening public life.

More about the Kettering Foundation can be found at www.kettering.org